THE GIFT OF COLLABORATIVE FEEDBACK

Illustrations by David Lewis

Cover Design and typesetting by www.bookstyle.co.uk

Printed in Great Britain by KDP

A CIP catalogue record for this book is available from the British Library

ISBN 978-1-9161860-0-2

THE GIFT OF COLLABORATIVE FEEDBACK

Transforming the way we talk in the workplace

CHRIS CHIN

To assist organizations and individuals improve their
Collaborative Feedback skills, please visit
the following website:

www.curiouslearning.co.uk

CONTENTS

COLLABORATIVE FEEDBACK

What if there was an approach to deliver feedback in such a way so as to be almost irresistible to others? A way that sends a compelling invitation – that opens doors to productive conversations and that achieves the outcomes we want?
This core skill profoundly affects the success of every individual both in and out of the workplace. And as a result organizations thrive or shrivel depending on how well it's collectively done. It's at the heart of communication, learning and our ability to get on with others. This skill is what I call 'Collaborative Feedback' – our ability to feedback information, which engages others around us – to adapt – so that we can collectively go where we want to go. Collaborative feedback allows us to co-create together as human beings – to be the very best that we all can be. You might like to think of Collaborative Feedback as the bridge from noticing what could be better - to productive and generative conversations. I hope you enjoy this book.

INTRODUCTION

WHY COLLABORATIVE FEEDBACK

It was Friday afternoon, and we had just finished a staff meeting. I was about to go when my boss asked me to stay behind for a few minutes.

'Can I give you some feedback on your performance with the clients?'

Inside I gulped a little but said, 'Of course.'

'You need to pick up your performance. You need to have more impact on the clients.'

I thought, *OK... I'm doing my best*, but I didn't say anything. At that time, any kind of input put me in a rabbit-in-the-headlight state. I needed time to process.

My boss proceeded to give me input, and I continued, I'm sure, to appear unresponsive – but now more like a confused baby rabbit in a hypnotic trance. After a while, she paused and said, 'I don't know what it is exactly about you. You don't take feedback onboard. In fact, you come across as being a bit slimy!'

Now I'm pretty sure she didn't mean 'slimy' - maybe slippery or defensive; it wasn't perhaps what she intended to say, but the word slipped out anyway – and I'm also sure she was trying to be helpful because she was that kind of person. However, I have no recollection of whatever else followed because my mind shut down after her comment, as did my relationship with her.

Slimy? Slimy?? Slimy??? What the hell?

I consider myself to be a reasonably logical, not overly emotional, kind of a guy but shortly after I left there followed tears of anger at being labelled 'slimy', tears of regret for not giving a cutting response and tears of shame for allowing the situation to happen. Feedback? Minefield! Boom! Another rabbit bites the dust (although no animals were harmed).

More on this story later...

What this book is about

The Gift of Collaborative Feedback is all about encouraging two-way interaction in feedback (unlike my example above) – a co-creation, if you like between the giver and receiver – so you can make something even better, and get somewhere, that you might not get to on your own. Of course, you can give feedback in lots of different ways; you might not have time for, or even want, a two-way interaction. You're still giving feedback, but it won't necessarily be collaborative.

Collaborative Feedback is all about encouraging a two-way interaction in feedback to co-create something even better

This book is specifically about Collaborative Feedback – feedback that is much more likely to end in a collaborative effort. It's useful because often, there's 'stuff' that others see, that we don't, but when we combine our perspectives, something different emerges – usually a way forward that resonates with both parties. Sounds appealing, doesn't it? Or is it La La Land? (Love that musical! And by 'love', I mean 'quite like'.) But the reality of feedback is that it isn't always like that, is it? And I'm sure that you too have you been a victim of poorly delivered feedback at one time or another. Perhaps from your boss? A colleague? Your parents? A family member? Or even a well-meaning friend?

Alternatively, have you ever given feedback and then

wished you could stuff the words right back into your mouth because you know what you've said is going to cause problems? (Perhaps as you watched them walk away with a stoic face – hiding their pain, frustration, anger, tears.) I have. In fact, more times than I care to remember.

Have you ever had feedback thrown at you in the form of an innocuous comment and the giver walks away seemingly oblivious, leaving you confused, dazed and a little bit hurt? A small comment that feels more like a big grenade – maybe the intention was well-meaning, but it did more harm than good. Or have you ever had a friend moaning or crying about some criticism or personal attack from a manager or colleague after a brutal day's work? They've discovered they've been labelled as a 'troublemaker'? Not a team player? Or any other undesirable label? If you're an average human who's ever worked in an organization of any kind, you probably know what I'm talking about.

Feedback is a necessary part of everyday life. One of my experienced colleagues calls feedback a 'kill skill'. I'm not sure I would use those words, but I know what she means. Your ability, and the quality, with which you give feedback is hugely important. Feedback helps us grow, improve and maintain standards; it enables course correction, and it also plays a vital part in living peacefully with one another. When someone violates your values or morals, we must point it out and resolve it, or the relationship may break in some way. It's also business critical. When someone violates an organization's standard, ethic or simply underperforms, we must address it. If we don't, we inevitably erode some key process, connection or way of working. Our value proposition diminishes, and we end up leaving money on the table. Silence may be the best tactic at the time, but if it continues to be an issue, it can become a ticking time bomb. Feedback lies at the heart of collaboration and prosperous and peaceful coexistence.

This is all very well, but we both know that giving feedback can sometimes be tricky. But it's often these situations where giving feedback is the most necessary. That's why learning to give skilful feedback is one of life's most valuable skills and can make a tremendous difference to both your home and work life.

Below is a brief questionnaire that I'd like you to answer:

1. Do you feel nervous about giving feedback to someone more senior than you in your organization?
2. Does giving feedback rarely cross your mind?
3. Do you, from time to time, find yourself in an argument or heated disagreement and wonder, how did that happen?
4. Do you find yourself giving feedback and the conversation goes off course and you end up feeling like your feedback hasn't been heard?
5. Do you feel like less senior colleagues in your organization give you compliant responses rather than engage on a real level?
6. Do you find seemingly simple problems in your organization hard to remove?
7. Do you have difficulty knowing what to do to fix rifts in relationships at work?
8. Do you feel anxious about having tricky conversations at work?
9. Do you find that nobody seems to hear what you have to say but don't know how to change it?

10. Do you feel that people (perhaps one particular person) fobs you off with superficial answers, but you don't know how to proceed without offending them?
11. Do you find yourself freezing or reacting in unhelpful ways when you unexpectedly receive challenging feedback?
12. Do you need to say some things but feel you can't because it would be inappropriate?
13. Do you find others reacting in unexpected ways to the feedback you give?
14. Do you find the 'wrong' words seem to pop out of your mouth when you are trying to give challenging feedback to someone else in a tricky situation?
15. Do you feel caught in a no-win situation because of the feedback you think you need to give?
16. Do you feel defensive, or on the back foot, when someone gives you challenging feedback?
17. Do you feel like there's often no point in giving feedback because it causes more problems than it solves?
18. Do you find conversations in meetings going around in circles but don't know how to address the issue without coming across as being 'difficult'?
19. Do you find people go quiet on you after giving feedback, when instead you would like a coaching conversation?

If you answered yes to three or more of these questions, then you'll undoubtedly find this book helpful.

I've been running a company called Curious Learning for nearly two decades, delivering programs and courses designed to help leaders and managers develop their workforces. One theme which continually springs up is that people are nervous about giving feedback to others – so much so, that I've developed techniques specifically focused on the delivery of feedback. As part of their development, program participants deliver lots of feedback, and I ask them to focus on two things:

- What did you say and do?
- What specifically were the responses and results you got?

I ask them to capture their conversations, and then we look at the effects of the feedback they gave.

Successful collaboration usually leads to better outcomes and, over the years, we've spotted patterns of speech and behaviours that lead to success – and those that don't. We've extracted principles from these observations and then created a simple tool that enables most people to hugely increase the effectiveness of their feedback conversations. And that's the purpose of this book: to share our discoveries with you.

I'm not going to say that giving feedback will always be comfortable, even if you do put the principles into practice. In fact, any nervousness and/or apprehension before giving tricky feedback is usually a signal that you need to take extra care in preparing it – there's a relationship or something more at stake. But understanding the principles and engaging in the practices will make it easier and give you more confidence, because you'll know what's happening at every stage and can keep adjusting your delivery.

Many participants on my programs have commented that whereas they once dreaded giving feedback to others, they now actually enjoy it and are much more confident about giving and receiving feedback. So, the goal of this book is to hugely increase your capability for having tricky conversations with those around you, and in such a way that the relationship grows.

This book is primarily for those who work in the corporate world. In particular, it's aimed at those of you who have management responsibilities. But if you work in an organization of any size and have to deal with colleagues or clients, then this book is also for you because you'll soon discover that feedback isn't just about business or work; it finds its way into different areas of your life – family, friends, anyone you have a relationship with. That's because feedback is an inbuilt mechanism in every interaction you have with others. It's a core part of communication and getting what you want from life.

I also wanted this book to be very informal, and a simple read because I suspect those with management responsibilities are short of time. Although it was written with a lot of psychological research in mind, I've purposely only touched on the theory. Instead, I hope the examples and principles resonate with you and that you test them out by trial and error. You'll also probably notice that, from time to time, I repeat concepts I've covered previously. This is in line with one of the objectives of the book: by the end of reading it, you'll have a firm grasp on how to use the principles.

I'm confident if you open your eyes to what feedback really is, you'll find plenty of opportunities to test it out. As you'll discover, Collaborative Feedback is a gift and should be delivered and received as such.

Hanna was delighted when she discovered feedback was a gift and not a kick in the teeth.

How to use this book

If you're already confident in giving feedback, understand the importance of giving and receiving feedback, and just looking for ways to improve your delivery, feel free to go straight to Chapter 3 onward, where you can explore the principles of successful feedback, followed by the PRESENT Model of Collaborative Feedback and its subsequent implementation. However, I'm confident that the insights in the earlier chapters will also impact your thinking.

In Chapter 1, we'll explore why it's essential to get skilled at giving and receiving feedback. Unless we see and feel the need to improve, most people never take the time to properly learn or develop this valuable skill. Then in Chapter 2, we'll delve into the problems that can arise when giving and receiving feedback, such as:

- How often we don't realize we are giving feedback.
- Other people's reactions when they feel criticized.
- The inability to think clearly during tricky feedback.
- The underlying problem – the right to give feedback.
- How language can be easily misinterpreted and the stories that arise consequently.
- The different modes of communication which can cause confusion.

In Chapter 3, we'll look at the elements of successful feedback which are often present when feedback works well. We'll look at why these are important and how the feedback process can be derailed when they are missing. Chapter 4 describes the PRESENT Model of Collaborative Feedback and is followed by the presentation of a super simple, useful tool that will help you prepare your feedback in Chapter 5. Chapter 6 gives practical tips for how to deliver feedback successfully and answers some of the issues often experienced when adopting this new methodology.

Chapter 7 addresses how to maximize 'positive' feedback and its potential to change corporate culture for the better. Chapter 8 then explores how to receive feedback. Let's face it, there will always be people who aren't very good at giving feedback. What if you had a way to unpack their intention and get clarity on exactly what they are saying? How useful would that be?

In Chapter 9, we'll look at the broader implications of using the Collaborative Feedback Model as a tool because you may be surprised how versatile it is in other areas of your life – which you might not strictly label as feedback.

And finally, in the Conclusion, we'll summarize our journey and look briefly at how to go about creating a culture of Collaborative Feedback in your workplace.

The goal of this book is to equip you to deliver feedback more efficiently, effectively and even elegantly. You'll discover that feedback creeps into multiple areas of life that you might not have recognized. In becoming more self-aware, you'll automatically know how to avoid inadvertently causing problems. If this is something you hope to attain from this book, here's some advice obtained from nearly two decades of training this stuff:

It will take a short period of sustained practice, trial and error before Collaborative Feedback feels natural.

Also, you'll probably need to adjust the way you prepare for feedback and tinker with some of your language patterns. Think of it like learning to play tennis or basketball or any other sport. The theory is easy, but actually playing takes practice before it 'feels' elegant and natural. As a result, you need never fear giving or receiving feedback ever again. Perhaps you'll even look forward to those situations and see them as an opportunity to deepen your relationships.

Finally, a quick note, throughout this book, I've used real-life examples to illustrate the various points. These examples came from people who were generous enough to share them with me in confidence, and I am deeply grateful to them for doing so and, for that reason, I have taken the liberty of changing most of their names. I sincerely hope you enjoy our time together.

CHAPTER 1

THE IMPORTANCE OF FEEDBACK

I think you'd be surprised if you thought about how often we give feedback. Sometimes we are giving feedback and don't even realize we're doing so. Think about a time when you bounced in with a great idea about something, and it was met with a brief silence followed by a stilted, "Yeah...that sounds great." Whether they knew it or not, you had been 'feedbacked'. Boom! Feedback is one of life's necessities – from addressing broken promises to negotiating different expectations – and we need to get good at it.

I've known quite a few people who have spent their lives trying to avoid getting feedback for fear of what they might hear. And yes, I've been one of those people at various points in my life. I remember one occasion when I literally stuck my fingers in my ears, like I was six instead of forty-six, and hummed to block out the wise words my wife had for me – after I had neglected to do something I'd promised. As you can imagine, that conversation did not end well. (I've seen Homer Simpson do something similar!) And another observation: people who tend to avoid getting feedback, often give it out much less. They figure, because of the way they feel about it, that others don't want to hear it either. They don't see that feedback is a gift. It's always a gift (of sorts) – even if the feedback is inaccurate. We'll talk about why this is so a bit later.

So, in this chapter, we'll explore the meaning of Collaborative Feedback and through several contexts, when and why it's essential to give feedback.

Defining Collaborative Feedback will give you an insight into its strategic, practical use. Exploring 'when' will enable you to recognize opportunities to provide feedback and exploring 'why' will provide you with the conviction to prepare and give feedback. We'll do this by looking at a variety of different scenarios in which feedback is necessary for the workplace; these include:

- Producing clarity
- Establishing ways of working
- Ensuring commitment from colleagues
- Ensuring standards and quality
- People development
- Performance management
- Relationships with management
- Negotiations
- Counteracting hierarchical power structures
- Feedback as a source of motivation and energy
- Clients and customers
- Conversations with colleagues

Finally, in this chapter, we'll look very briefly at the uses of feedback beyond the work environment, of which there are many; these include:

- Personal relationships
- Friends

- Children
- Parents
- Neighbors
- Service providers

Defining feedback

Let's start off by getting on the same page by describing the meaning of feedback. The *Oxford English Dictionary* has a couple of definitions; they are:

- Information about reactions to a product, a person's performance of a task, etc., which is used as a basis for improvement.
- The modification or control of a process or system by its results or effects, for example, in a biochemical pathway or behavioural response.

For the purposes of this book, I'm going to lean toward the first definition as I think it lends itself better to what I'd like to explore.

On a personal basis, feedback is simply information or data that is fed back, so that you can have more perspective on where you are, in line with a goal or objective you may have. With this knowledge, you can decide to keep going or change course. Feedback is simply information or data. We can further define feedback by categorizing it into two types:

- Affirmational feedback (often termed positive feedback)
- Adjustment feedback (often termed negative or constructive feedback)

Personally, I don't like the use of 'positive' and 'negative feedback' because 'negative' or even 'critical' feedback has unhelpful, widely held, connotations. People, in organizations everywhere naturally translate positive as good and negative as bad, even though the original labels are more about amplification and reduction of behaviours. All feedback is positive or constructive in the sense that it is useful, even when we don't agree with it. Feedback gives us another person's perspective on where we are with a goal or objective and helps us modify our behaviours accordingly. At the very least, it can broaden our minds to a different perspective and the bigger picture. The terms affirmational feedback and adjustment feedback may be unfamiliar to many organizations, but they much better describe the function of the two types of feedback, and from now on, in this book, those are the terms I'll use.

So, for clarity:

- Adjustment feedback = negative / constructive feedback
- Affirmational feedback = positive feedback

Adjustment feedback is given when the information suggests you might need to change course in some way. Affirmational feedback is given to reinforce a way of thinking, doing or being. Adjustment feedback is, for example: 'I think you might need to consider changing something. It's not going as well or as efficiently as it could be.' Affirmational feedback is, for example: 'Hey, you're doing great already. Keep going.'

Juan had to course correct because he found he was travelling in the wrong direction.

There are rarely problems with giving and receiving affirmational feedback. Even if it's delivered unskilfully, it won't generally cause problems. After all, how much harm can a 'well done' do? My opinion, from working with many different organizations, is that we probably don't give enough affirmational feedback. Of course, you might be the exception to the rule, and if that's the case, I urge you to carry on or even calm down a bit! In my experience, affirmational feedback is significantly underutilized, and I've devoted a whole chapter to make a case for expanding its use and the way that it's delivered in organizations.

Isabella gave herself a pat on the back because she was headed right for the target.

On the other hand, there are lots of dangers with giving adjustment feedback as we'll explore in the following chapter. But before we get into these, let's look at why we should be looking for opportunities to give all kinds of feedback.

There are lots of reasons why it's crucial to give adjustment and affirmational feedback both at work and outside of work – some of these are obvious, and some are not. And there are significant consequences that can come back and bite us when we avoid giving and taking onboard feedback. We'll explore some of these later in the chapter.

Defining Collaborative Feedback

You can give feedback with a collaborative intent or a non-collaborative intent. The *Oxford English Dictionary* defines collaboration as 'the action of working with someone to produce something'. I think of it as co-creation. You can simply throw information or data at someone – to do what they will with it (I call this 'dump and run') – or deliver it in such a way as to co-create something between you. I believe this is where the power is; when we truly work together to produce something even better. Even affirmational feedback can be collaborative. Then, it's not just about 'well done; keep going' – it's a powerful way of modelling practices to improve performance for the individual and for the organization. More on this in Chapter 7.

You'll probably discover the way I define and use the word 'feedback' is slightly broader than its general use in most organizations. When we explore the different contexts, you'll see why.

Feedback in the workplace

If you've ever worked in an organization, you'll probably know things get done as a result of a conversation somewhere. And if it's to be done well, it's probably true the conversation needs to have clarity. Think of all the times when a project hasn't gone well, because of misunderstandings. Clarity ensues when effective feedback processes are being employed by those conversing. All communication depends on quality feedback loops. Without these loops, we wouldn't know if others have heard us or if they've heard us correctly.

Producing clarity

I can't tell you the number of times I've come away from an Executive Team meeting and everyone thinks they are on the same page regarding a vision, strategy or initiative. But when I ask for details from the participants afterwards, it's clear there are often significant differences in understanding. And that's mainly because team members are not feeding back their understanding into the conversation enough, because they assume that everyone knows what they are saying. And when they subsequently try to deliver on their 'agreement', it invariably results in work being done inefficiently, ineffectively or even having to be redone. The entire organization suffers as a result. This is why giving feedback and receiving feedback are essential components of clear communication.

Establishing ways of working

Feedback is essential for developing ways of working. Here follows an example of what I mean. I remember having a conversation with one of my colleagues a few years ago about the way we talked to each other. My colleague is a natural-born storyteller. He has a story for everything and loves to go into detail so that his stories come to life. I, on the other hand, like to keep things simple. It drives me mad when people take forever to get to the point. Here's how the conversation went:

> CHRIS: I've noticed that whenever I ask you a question, you tell me a detailed story about something, and it takes way more time than necessary to get to the point. Do you think we could change that? I mean, I like your stories and all, but not all the time.

COLLEAGUE: Ah, well, that's probably because I have a passion for telling stories and how they enrich other people's lives. My father—

CHRIS: You're doing it again.

COLLEAGUE: Am I? Well, interestingly, a few years ago, I had a conversation with another colleague who brought up the same thing. He said… *[cue another story]*.

CHRIS: *[Doh!]*

Feedback conversations are necessary regarding the way we go about doing things. We all have different preferences and values, and if we don't establish a 'common' preferred method of working, we'll be fighting to keep the annoyance at bay. I regularly see people compromising in their interactions because they haven't had the conversations and figured out a new different way!

Ensuring commitment from others

Good, quality feedback is essential for ownership and commitment. If you've ever served on a leadership or management team, you know you need to get your staff onboard if your strategy or initiative is going to succeed. Without them, you won't be able to successfully deliver. They need to take some form of ownership, and you need to know if they are really committing. Unless people feedback into the strategy, ownership and commitment are unlikely to happen. You lose clarity, energy and ultimately the vision of where you are going.

Ensuring standards and quality

You also need feedback to enforce standards. As a business, you've implicitly or explicitly promised a set of standards to your customers and your staff to deliver a value proposition. To make sure these standards are maintained, feedback must be given in many directions- upwards, sideways, downwards. It may be that your staff aren't focusing on the right things. It may be that processes have key gaps. It may be that your customers expect too much, too fast. It may even be, you as the leader have made some fundamental strategic errors! All this needs to be handled with successful, Collaborative Feedback.

Feedback for personal development

You need to ensure your people are developing in line with the needs of the organization and its chosen market. For the organization to improve, we need to continually challenge each other to grow; be more efficient; be more productive. This only happens with constant, continual feedback. Even for simple things – here's what I mean:

A few years ago, I was working with a senior leadership team on a development program and one of the directors, who was sitting next to me, was preparing a presentation on PowerPoint. I couldn't help but notice she was copying and pasting the company logo many times to keep the branding consistent. It occurred to me she probably didn't know about creating a master slide which would save her a significant amount of time. So, I gave her some feedback – delivered in a collaborative sense. She was immensely grateful for the help. It saved her a great deal of time and eased the pressure off her already crazy work schedule!

How many of us see these little things in the workplace but hesitate to give feedback, because we think it's not our place or our colleagues might not react well and how many thousands of work hours are wasted by inefficient work processes because we hold back? Why is it that most people who are using popular software like Word, Excel or PowerPoint are at the same level 20 years later? Surely that's not right. After 20 years, everyone should be kind of in the expert zone, right?

Performance management

Whatever performance management system you're using to motivate, measure and reward your people, feedback will be a critical component. It doesn't matter if you're doing a half-yearly/annual appraisal system or a more modern, continual assessment type system, your managers will have to get comfortable with delivering quality feedback. With certain types of appraisal systems, I often hear employees complaining when they don't get the results they are expecting. 'Why wasn't I told this earlier? It's not fair!' No one, in my opinion, should ever be surprised by what is said at the appraisal conversation – that's just bad practice. It causes so many problems, including grumbling, low morale and even turnover of staff. It's in everyone's interest that they know how they are performing throughout the year – it's just common sense.

I was chatting to one relatively new staff member of a bank, who had been working there for six months. He was feeling very insecure about how he had been doing. When I asked him why this was, it transpired that he had only ever had one person give him any kind of feedback as to how he measured up to company standards.

I remember having another conversation with a manager in an organization about the performance of one of her direct reports (let's call him Oliver). She wasn't particularly happy with how Oliver was presenting his sales pitches, and this was shown by his results. When I asked how often she gave him feedback and coaching the conversation went like this:

CHRIS: How often do you give him feedback and coach him through it?

MANAGER: Not very often, but I have mentioned that he needs to do better.

CHRIS: What's your reason for not giving him feedback?

MANAGER: I don't know really. I think people in the business are afraid to give feedback to each other because it's caused problems in the past and is perceived as a bit negative now. We need to keep things positive.

CHRIS: So, what happens if nothing changes?

MANAGER: Well, he'll keep failing.

CHRIS: And how will that impact you?

MANAGER: It'll affect the reputation of my team and my leadership

After a little bit of coaching, she started giving feedback and coaching, and Oliver's results improved dramatically.

Any innovations or improvement of processes cannot happen without feedback. In fact, any change initiative requires copious amounts of feedback. We live in dynamic systems that continually change and evolve, and without quality feedback, our attempts to improve will fail.

Giving feedback to your manager

One thing I commonly notice in organizations – which just doesn't make sense – is the lack of feedback given from direct reports to their managers. I was talking to a group of regional directors during a coffee break, and the topic came up about getting feedback from the people they managed. One of the directors responded: 'Oh, God, no. That would open a massive can of worms.'

When I asked them, 'How do you know how to get the best out of your reports if you aren't getting information from them as to how to do it?' I got a few nods and a few blank stares.

In the organizations I've worked with, this is not an unusual mindset. How 'normal' is it for reports to give feedback to their managers? (And I'm not talking about cocky new upstarts who know very little but think they know everything.) The relationship between manager and reports works best when it's symbiotic – meaning they work together to achieve the best outcome. It makes a manager's job much harder if the input is primarily one way.

Look at the following example:

Annette was John's manager in a housing association. Annette thought John was competent and adopted a hands-off management style giving John free reign. When John asked for direction about something, her deliberate answer was, 'Figure it out.' In her mind, she was trying to help him improve his problem-solving skills. This left John incredibly frustrated, and after a year of this type of dynamic, John decided to leave. When I talked to him, the conversation went like this:

CHRIS: Why did you leave?

JOHN: I really liked working there. The work was meaningful, but I got so frustrated with my manager. She didn't care, and she didn't help with hardly anything – no direction whatsoever.

CHRIS: Did you have a conversation about this?

JOHN: I tried telling her my frustrations, but she just kept saying, 'Figure it out yourself.'

CHRIS: Had you considered that she really believes in you?

JOHN: Yes, but it wasn't helping me.

CHRIS: Did you feed that back to her?

JOHN: It's not my place to give my manager feedback about her management style... And to be seen to be criticizing my manager wouldn't go down well with senior management.

When I talked to Annette, she was confused, frustrated and disappointed that John had decided to leave because she thought they had got on well together.

CHRIS: Did he ever talk to you about his frustrations?

ANNETTE: Not really. He did ask me how he should get things done, but I thought it would be more helpful for him in the long term if he tried to figure it out himself and then we could review how it went and what could have gone better.

CHRIS: And how did those review conversations go?

ANNETTE: Well, they never happened because things got hectic at the organization.

CHRIS: Did John ever give you any feedback about the way your relationship was going?

ANNETTE: Not really. He would just get on with it. But if he had, I would have been more than willing to listen.

Both John and Annette were well-intentioned, but both lost out due to not having those critical feedback conversations.

Feedback in negotiations

If you ever need to negotiate in your role, it's immensely useful to give feedback to the other party, or parties, you are negotiating with. Why? Because feedback creates clarity, relieves tensions and can also call out any unhelpful behaviours that may hinder an acceptable agreement for everyone. And it's possible to call these out in a respectful manner – in a way that will build and not harm the relationship. It helps negotiations become more transparent and can reduce the power games that are played. More about this in a later chapter.

Feedback eliminates power

And this leads us to the next point. Skilful Collaborative Feedback has the side effect of eliminating unnecessary power.

What do I mean by this?

In any social structure – organizations, families, circle of friends – power structures exist. In these social structures, pecking orders are determined and maintained, but often, these invisible pecking orders get in the way of progress and achieving the desired results. People 'feel' these hierarchies, and it stops them from saying what they need to say. I've seen competent directors crumble into inarticulate 'idiots' (their words, not mine) because of the power dynamic between them and their CEO. I've seen leadership teams avoid asking critical questions and then watched their strategy fail because of the power dynamic.

This is not good for businesses, because it hinders information from flowing up, down and sideways in an organization. People stop talking. And if people stop talking 'things' stop happening and ultimately the business is held back from being what it could be.

But when staff confidently and collaboratively give feedback, power seems to dissipate in service to broader business goals. As a result, engagement increases, as does satisfaction, wellbeing and results. Power is an illusion and only exists if we give it credence, but it's a powerful illusion; one felt in our bones. Giving feedback skilfully and collaboratively works to begin to dissolve the illusion.

The CEO Alessandro didn't realize the power his words and tone held and was frequently surprised at the defense systems he encountered.

Feedback as a source of motivation and best practice

Let's talk about affirmational feedback in the workplace – one of my personal bugbears. As I mentioned earlier in the chapter, affirmational feedback is massively underutilized. I have lots of conversations with senior leaders searching for ways to incentivize staff – to find ways to motivate the workforce. I make it a point when I work with businesses, to ask employees how often they receive affirmational feedback for a job well done. The answer, all too often, is – not enough. Imagine what it would be like working in an organization where the large majority of people are skilfully giving affirmational feedback in a unclichéd manner? I've seen it in a handful of organizations, and the difference it makes to morale and productivity is stunning.

One of the most effective and greatest ways to make employees feel valued is by giving good quality, affirmational feedback. When done well and consistently, it produces a great working atmosphere. When was the last time someone came up to you and got very specific about what you were doing well? We'll talk about how to do this in Chapter 7.

Feedback to clients and customers

From time to time, you have to give feedback to your clients and customers. Why? Because if you don't, they may hold unrealistic expectations and continue to indulge in behaviours that may hurt your business.

Occasionally, my business, Curious Learning, is required to work in the change management space. Organizations hire us to help them to implement change initiatives. Our clients are usually senior teams. Sometimes these same top teams who hire us, behave in ways that work against the changes they are looking for. Unless they alter some of their own behaviours, the changes they want are unlikely to be sustainable – and this hurts what we do. To get the senior teams to change, we must be able to give them feedback that engages them and encourages them to improve their own behaviours.

Feedback to co-workers

Most of us work with others. We have to collaborate together. Unfortunately, from time to time, individuals will display behaviours that annoy you. Most of us put up with these as a necessary evil of getting on together, but often feedback and a fruitful discussion can sort these out.

I have the habit of sometimes finishing other people's sentences, which drives my finance director up the wall. She will often pause mid-sentence, look at me and then wait for me to say, 'Sorry, I'm assuming things again, aren't I?' before continuing.

I have a close business associate and friend who is brilliant in many ways. He can command the complete attention of large crowds in business conferences, has an incredible ability to engage people with his storytelling and uses humour as a precursor to in-depth communication. He's also got a great business brain. But he sometimes wanders off course when we are in a project meeting or a conference call. In my mind, what could take 10 minutes turns into half-an-hour. When I finally plucked up the courage to give him feedback about this, it was quickly sorted out, and we found a different way of working together. How many meetings are we in, where conversations wander around and around in circles, and we end up not achieving our objective? What a massive waste of our precious time.

Only when we address these sorts of things by giving skilful feedback can we hope to find a pleasant, productive, coexistence in the workplace.

Many organizations underestimate the importance of feedback to their own detriment. They don't address poor quality feedback, underutilize affirmational feedback and inadvertently allow the avoidance of feedback. Then they wonder why problems continue to exist, why innovation is low, and why things are resistant to change.

One insightful CEO of a dynamic consultancy I worked with didn't fall into this way of thinking and drove hard to have every employee go through feedback and coaching training. He recognized that his employees becoming proficient at feedback was essential for the health and competitiveness of the organization. If they were to grow as a business, everyone had to improve, and feedback is critical for that to happen. As they went through the training, a large proportion of the participants commented on how they had underestimated the importance of feedback in so many areas.

Feedback outside the workplace

Whether we recognize it as feedback or not, we need to give feedback outside of the workplace too. Since this is primarily a book about giving feedback at work, we won't spend too long on this. But the fact is, we all have lives outside our workplaces.

When we run our feedback programs in organizations, a lot of the examples and situations that people put forward are non-work specific – after all, it's all feedback. We'll look at a few of these areas.

Feedback in relationships

In any relationship, no matter how perfect they seem initially, my bet is, some things might possibly annoy you. Am I right?

I'm married to Karen and rest assured there are lots of things I do that annoy her. One of these was the way I tidied up. We had different standards. My version of tidy was if you looked around the room and there was a reasonable amount of tidy space – well, that would simply do! Karen's version is a bit more involved. Everything in our house has a place and if it's not in that place... well, you can't describe it as tidy.

Once she came back from work, and I noticed the look on her face as she looked around the room.

CHRIS: What?

KAREN: I thought we'd agreed that you would tidy up the place, as I was getting home a bit later than you?

CHRIS: It is tidy.

KAREN: How?

CHRIS: Look around. The floor is clear, and the dishes are done

KAREN: [*Looking around the room and pointing at objects.*] Well that doesn't belong there, and that doesn't belong there, and if you open that cupboard, I'm sure that you'll find its topsy-turvy and lots of things don't belong in there

CHRIS: What, so you have x-ray vision now?

That comment didn't go down well either!

There are lots of things we must feedback to one another and work on if the relationship is to flourish. From putting the toilet seat down, to dishwashing standards, how to manage the finances and the list goes on and on. In fact, recognize that anytime you have an argument with someone else, you are, in a way, giving feedback. You are suggesting what they are thinking is wrong and needs to change.

We all hold different values and rules associated with these values, and when these values are stepped on, they cause us a little bit of pain. If not addressed, these little pains compile into something more significant.

Feedback with friends

There are times when we must have tricky conversations with friends too. I've seen so many friendships dissolve because irritating behaviours aren't addressed. Sometimes our friends impinge too much on our time or too little, which can cause friction. But if we want them to remain, good friends, we need to have these adjustment conversations. Sometimes perspectives or priorities change. My wife runs a cancer charity and many sufferers' outlook on life changes during treatment, which can affect their relationships. Friends don't realize the extent to which perspectives and expectations change and carry on as usual, which becomes irritating or distressing to the person going through cancer. If sensitive feedback doesn't occur, it can destroy long term friendships.

Feedback with children

Our children need lots of feedback as they navigate their childhood and teen years – and beyond. They need feedback on their education, on morals, on how to navigate the complex social environment of the playground, and the list goes on. And I'm pretty sure most parents aren't shy in giving that feedback. But is the feedback useful? Does it get the intended results, and is it done in a way that builds up our children's self-confidence and makes them feel secure?

Are we talking about the right things? The things that really matter. And in a way that our children really listen and are influenced? I've noticed a big difference when I take care to prepare the feedback with my children, and when I don't.

Feedback with parents

It doesn't matter how old you are – it's often tricky having to address issues with our parents. And let's face it, we need to. One thing I've noticed is that our parents often tend to treat us as younger than we really are. I remember a conversation that occurred with my mum a few years ago when I travelled back up to see her and my dad:

> MUM: Chris, it's cold. Put on a sweater.
>
> CHRIS: Yeah, I'm kind of fortyish. I think I know when to put on a sweater.
>
> MUM: Put one on.
>
> CHRIS: OK.

As a dad of two children, one currently 20 and the other 16, I also recognize I'm sometimes slow to adapt to change. I can no longer treat them like they are ten years younger and sometimes don't realize that I am doing this. My daughter often tells me, 'Stop cracking your stupid dad jokes. They're not funny and, in fact, they're embarrassing.' I'm afraid at this point – no amount of feedback is going to make that happen!

Parents often moan that their children are just 'being teens'. Could it be that our teens are just giving us unskilful feedback? Or, more controversially, perhaps we as parents don't know how to process feedback from a place of power?

My kids have often given me feedback, which has ended up in arguments because I'm reacting to the way they deliver it. 'I'm your dad, and you shouldn't be talking to me in that way!' The power I hold as a parent sometimes grips me, and as a result, I don't listen – and yes, that's mostly my fault (feedback person – teach thyself). And so, to fellow parents, what if we teach our children how to give us feedback skilfully – in a way that gets results with us? It sends a powerful empowerment message to our children and makes for more peaceful households!

Feedback with neighbours

We want the areas where we live to be great. Our neighbours sometimes unwittingly indulge in antisocial behaviour, and we need to find ways to address these. I'm pretty sure some won't respond to feedback however skilfully you give it, but there will be occasions where giving feedback in a non-inflammatory manner can be hugely helpful. One of our neighbours, Emily, has had an ongoing 20-year dispute with the people next door. It's very frosty and unpleasant and, from time to time, erupts into full-blown verbal exchanges. Emily and Ann had been good friends for several years. The dispute started because Ann had a big tree, and the branches began growing over the fence into Emily's property. Emily promptly clipped them and gently threw the clippings back over the fence as was her right. When Ann saw what Emily had done, she knocked on Emily's door and proceeded to give her some ill-prepared feedback. And so, began the 20-year saga, which now continues into the next generation. Who knows what would have happened if different words were chosen and the feedback delivered in a slightly different way?

Feedback with service providers

Whether it's dealing with utility providers, workmen or shopkeepers who short-change us, it's useful to be able to give skilful feedback.

I remember an incident I had with a satellite TV company a few years back. I had cancelled my subscription, and to my horror, I found out they had continued charging me for it. I rang up to complain and ranted at them for about 15 minutes. It only occurred to me afterwards that I was giving them feedback, and I had not thought about what I wanted as an outcome, nor the way I was going to get there. When we complain at any time, we are giving feedback – information to get an outcome.

I hope this chapter has helped you to begin to recognize the many scenarios in which feedback crops up. Not recognizing these scenarios, means we may miss the opportunity to give feedback to improve our organizations or our lives, or we may unwittingly give feedback without correctly preparing, leading to undesired consequences. Giving skilful feedback can make a big difference in many areas of our lives. In the next chapter, we'll begin to explore some of the issues with feedback.

Recap

- Feedback is simply information or data given about an outcome and can help modify behaviour.
- Collaborative Feedback is giving feedback with the intention of co-creating meaning together.
- Be aware when you are giving feedback.
- Feedback is an essential part of communication, so you need to get good at it.
- Feedback is essential for change, growth and innovation.
- Power affects feedback.
- Be aware of the many scenarios where feedback is necessary both inside and outside of work.

CHAPTER 2

THE PROBLEM WITH FEEDBACK

I've entitled this chapter 'The Problem with Feedback', but really it should be 'The Problem with Adjustment Feedback' – because it implies the recipient should change course in some way.

Affirmational feedback generally doesn't cause problems. As I said in the previous chapter, the issue with affirmational feedback is that it could be used much more powerfully. I've not come across many occasions where affirmational feedback causes pain and problems.

Having said that, I have come across incidences, where affirmational feedback causes irritation. (I like finding exceptions to the rule!) Let me give you an example. Juan was an experienced engineer in an organization and had worked there for many years. He had very little desire to go into management, but he was good at his job and had an excellent reputation. Robert, a young man in his late 20s, had recently joined the business and was assigned as Juan's manager. On one occasion, Robert gave Juan some affirmational feedback on a job well done, but the reaction was not what Robert expected. Juan seemed offended. In a management training session, Robert relayed the brief conversation to me:

ROBERT: Well done, Juan, that was really good.

JUAN: [*Speaking somewhat dismissively.*] My work is generally good.

ROBERT: Oh... OK. [*Looks somewhat awkward.*]

JUAN: Is there anything else?

ROBERT: Err… no.

Because I had a relationship with Juan, I was able to ask him about the interaction, and it turns out that he felt patronized by what Robert said. Now, you could probably argue other issues were going on with Juan regarding how he felt about management, but that's my point – there are often things going on, of which we aren't aware. Consequently, we need to prepare how we give feedback, even affirmational feedback.

Adjustment feedback is a different animal, though, and there are some fundamental issues with delivering adjustment feedback, which we'll explore below.

Trust and feedback

We want our feedback to be effective but, of course, that depends upon how well it is received. The relationship you have with the recipient plays an important role. If it is good and the levels of trust are high, your feedback is much more likely to be well received. Feedback can be given in an unskilful, even insensitive way, but if your relationship is good, the chances are, it still might work out fine. Then there are other situations in which no matter how skilfully the feedback is delivered, it rarely ends well because there is low trust between the giver and receiver.

Trust is critical in any kind of communication and affects understanding hugely. Let me demonstrate by doing a practical exercise with you.

Trust exercise

This exercise will take a couple of minutes. There are four parts:

Step 1

Close your eyes and think of someone you don't trust. Imagine having a conversation with them. As they are talking to you, what goes through your mind? Take a few seconds to do this now.

If you're anything like the many delegates in my programs who have done this, you'll find that as that imaginary person is talking, you have an active inner dialogue going on inside your mind – perhaps questioning, perhaps critiquing. Is that right? So, as they speak, you have two voices present. One is their voice speaking, and the other is your voice inside your head. Which one is louder?

The answer is clear – your voice. The implication of this is enormous. When levels of trust are low, we can't hear properly what other people are saying. Think about that. It's like having a conversation inside a crowded bar or nightclub. You can probably catch snippets of what they are saying, but not the whole thing. Oh, and that's perhaps not the only thing that's happening internally. Often the inner dialogue is accompanied by an uncomfortable feeling of anxiousness or discomfort in your body somewhere. So not only are you in a noisy, crowded bar or nightclub but you are with someone periodically poking you somewhere. How well are you able to focus now?

Incidentally, this is also why it's so essential for those of us involved in managing change in our organizations to be systematically communicating the same thing again and again. It's difficult to hear when there's lots of noise going on internally.

A few years ago I remember having a conversation with the director of an organization going through a significant change. The conversation went something like this:

DIRECTOR: They don't seem to be doing what we're asking them to do. They're stubborn and resistant. I guess people don't like change.

CHRIS: Do you think they understand what you're asking them to do?

DIRECTOR: They should do. We told them in the meeting, and their manager should have had the conversation with them about it too.

CHRIS: So, when you announced it, put yourself in their shoes. What do you think they thought as you announced it?

DIRECTOR: Probably wondering if their job was secure and a ton of other questions?

CHRIS: So, they've got a compelling inner narrative running on inside their head, probably accompanied by feelings of anxiousness? Is that right?

DIRECTOR: Yeah... I suppose.

CHRIS: Given that scenario, how likely are they to hear what you are saying?

DIRECTOR: Oh... wait... so are you saying they're too busy worrying about the future so they can't hear what we're telling them? So, they're not necessarily stubborn or resistant.

The penny then dropped: he realized the importance of bringing up the conversations again and again and again. By the way, I can't tell you the number of times I've had the same conversation with people in senior management positions in my consultancy work.

Let's move on to the second part of the exercise:

Step 2

This time close your eyes and think of someone you implicitly trust having a conversation with you. As they speak, what goes on inside your head now? Do the exercise right now.

Did you do it? What did you find? I bet that as you did the exercise this time around, you'll find there was probably silence as they spoke. It's like a library. You can hear a whisper. Everything is clear. It's much easier to hear. Am I right?

Now let's apply that specifically to feedback and not just a conversation.

Step 3

Close your eyes and think of someone you don't trust again. Imagine them giving some sort of feedback to you. As they are talking to you, what's going through your mind? Take a few seconds.

What's going on? Do you find you have a powerful inner dialogue going on inside – really questioning? Really critiquing. Things like, 'Really is that true? That's inaccurate. That's an assumption. Who are you to give me feedback? You're a hypocrite yourself...' and other similar things. Is that right?

How likely are you even to hear the feedback properly? If you're like me, you're already on the path of defending yourself or warding off the attack.

Step 4

Now one more time. Close your eyes and think of someone you implicitly trust giving you feedback. As they speak, what goes on inside your head?

What did you find this time? My bet is, as you did the exercise this time around, you'll find that your inner dialogue was a lot quieter and a lot less accusatory. Maybe there were questions, but you found it a lot quieter, and you were listening harder. There's a much better chance of you hearing what was said.

Trust is vital for successful feedback. For feedback to achieve its goal, it must be delivered in such a way that the intention is heard.

So, am I saying if the trust is low, you shouldn't give feedback? No, not at all. I'm just saying if trust is low, it's a lot trickier, and you must deliver it so much more skilfully. Even then, there's no guarantee it will be heard as you intended.

Aside from trust issues, there are several other reasons why adjustment feedback can be tricky:

The right to give feedback

There's a fundamental presupposition built into giving feedback; something which lurks beneath the surface – that is felt by nearly everyone: And it's this. 'What gives you the right to give feedback?'

Is it respectful in this scenario to give feedback? Can I give it? My colleague is presenting in a way I think is ineffective. Should I bring it up? That person, in my eyes, is dressed inappropriately. Can I bring it up? My neighbour is playing loud music. What gives me the right to dictate how they should behave?

In organizational life, this 'right' is often implicitly built into the hierarchy. My manager has the right to give me feedback as does anyone who sits on the senior management team. My mentor, if I have one, also has the right to give me feedback. But what about other colleagues? Suppliers? Customers? Clients?

The problems occur when one party in the feedback process thinks they have the right to give feedback, and the other party doesn't.

I also run a program for employees who are new to management. Frequently, the program participants have been promoted from the ranks. Individuals suddenly find themselves managers to those who were once their peers, which changes the dynamic of their relationship with their colleagues. They've established expectations and ways of working and now, suddenly, these must change. One of the most asked questions on my new to management program is 'How do I give feedback to people who were once my peers?' This dilemma often gives them great anguish, and they worry tremendously. They want to do well in their new role as manager but are fearful of losing their relationships or appearing aloof. The context has changed. The right to give a different level of feedback must be re-established.

If you have teenagers or children who are older, you're probably familiar with this situation too. Confused? Let me explain. I have a son who is now approaching 20 years old and lives at home. I often assume I have the right to give him feedback on, let's say, several issues. After all, I'm his dad. He unfortunately disagrees. (not that I'm his dad – but that I have the right to give feedback!) When I jump into giving adjustment feedback without establishing some sort of permission, it often ends badly.

As I described in the previous chapter, I'm sure I'm not alone in ongoing, persistent feedback from my mother – despite being in my 40s and 50s. I guess feedback is a gift that just keeps on giving!

This can be a tricky issue and can complicate communication. If we, as the giver of feedback, feel we don't have the right to give it, we experience an extra inner conflict that muddies our thinking. This then inevitably clouds the clarity in which we deliver the feedback.

The right to give adjustment feedback, if it isn't already established must be somehow built into the feedback process.

We are story-making machines

There's another fundamental problem with giving adjustment feedback, and it's this: as human beings, we create stories, and that brings issues – here's why. To give feedback, we first scan the environment for information. Then we process it and make a judgement call on what is important and what is not. We then create a story about it, and it's this story that informs us that we need to give feedback. Think about this carefully. It's hugely important. If we didn't go through this process, why do we need to give it in the first place?

There's a problem with this process though – actually, there are several issues with this. First and I'll yell this loudly... IT'S OUR STORY – a story we've created from our imagination. No matter how true that story seems to us, it's only one version. Second, the information we pick up is generally incomplete. There are always bits of information, both internal (what's going on inside people's heads) and external, that we cannot detect. And if we knew these bits of information, it might change our story. Finally, the judgement call that we make in our stories is based upon our values and not necessarily theirs. So, what do I mean by judgement call?

For example, I might look at a report and think it is badly written. What do I mean by badly written? What elements constitute badly written? Unless we have some sort of shared understanding of what a 'good' report looks like, we have difficulties.

So hopefully by now, we've established that we've created a story inside our minds – and there's nothing wrong with that – we're human. The problems arise when we share our story like it's the truth. I'll say that again in loud capital letters:

PROBLEMS ARISE WHEN WE SHARE OUR STORY LIKE IT'S THE TRUTH.

I remember one of my program participants (let's call him Bob) relaying a conversation to me about some feedback he'd received from his manager. Bob was asked by his manager to do a presentation to a room of senior leaders to pitch an initiative. Here's how the conversation went:

> MANAGER: You didn't perform well in that meeting, and your energy was low. The people in the room weren't engaged.
>
> BOB: Really? I'm not sure that's what happened...
>
> MANAGER: So, next time, you need to prepare better. Maybe we could run through your presentation beforehand so you perform well – as I know you can.

BOB: [*Silence.*]

See what's happening here? The manager is acting as if his perspective is the truth and, without listening, has moved on to the solutions. He's effectively saying, 'I know what the problems are. I know what the solutions are. So just do it.' I've seen so many people give feedback and immediately move on to provide a solution to the problem before the problem is even acknowledged and accepted.

If the problem isn't agreed, the solution won't be acted upon. Our initial feedback can never be the truth; it can only ever be our truth. And if we're not aware of how we are creating our stories, we will run into problems.

Likewise, we can't control how people process the information we offer them. As we provide our feedback, they're also simultaneously creating their own story of why and what is happening. They can make up the intent and inject meaning into things that weren't meant at all. If you give me feedback, I am taking the information you are communicating to me, and I am constructing a story. The problem for you as the giver of feedback is that you have very little control as to how and why I create my story inside my mind. Because of this, adjustment feedback won't be useful until the story we create as the feedback giver becomes a shared story.

It's somehow got to go from my story to our story.

Most people are not even aware they create their own stories to give feedback, but awareness of this must be a factor in an effective feedback process.

Sofia didn't realize her story had a different shape to that of her boss (and wondered why the two didn't fit).

Feedback is a dance, not a sprint

Sometimes participants on my feedback programs voice consternation that the principles they are learning don't work immediately: 'I prepared it like you suggested, but they were still resistant. See it doesn't work.'

I remember one manager who had delegated the running of an event to one of his colleagues, with the proviso, 'Come back and check with me before putting the plan into action.' He then found out to his immense annoyance, his colleague had already set things in motion without checking back and without realizing there were hidden consequences to the plan. 'That's the reason why I asked her to check back with me first,' the manager explained.

The manager had then planned to address the behaviour and taken the time to prepare the feedback. But, when he tried to deliver it sensitively, he found the colleague first misunderstanding his intentions and then misinterpreting the words and concluded, 'She's just not open to the feedback. The more I tried to explain, the more she reacted. It began to feel uncomfortable, so I stopped.'

What the manager hadn't realized is that this is what often happens in fruitful feedback conversations. And, rather like taking a swim in a pool on a hot day, people test the water and retest, until they decide it's OK to jump in.

The issue is that feedback is a dance – a back and forward, often circular, series of steps – and not a linear process like a sprint. Amos Tversky and Daniel Kahneman, in their work, for which Kahneman received a Nobel Prize in Economics (Tversky died six years earlier, and the prize isn't awarded posthumously), showed that people are often irrational in their thinking and processing of information.[1] Kahneman showed that human beings subjectively feel like they believe in something because they have arguments for it, but in fact, it's the other way around. They believe in the conclusion and then create supporting arguments. If we apply this to the way we, as humans, process information, feedback often isn't merely a straightforward linear, rational process of 'I give you the information. You look at what you can learn and adjust accordingly'. It is often a much more deeply instinctual and emotional process, which requires a back-and-forth iteration of listening, clarifying, assuring, listening reclarifying, reassuring – it's a dance, not a sprint. If you think it's a linear sprint then, at the first sign of deviation, you think it's going 'wrong, and you stop'. If you think it's a dance, then you simply move accordingly, knowing it's a normal part of the process.

Generalized language

This next reason is connected to the topic we've just covered. We've looked at how we create stories to give feedback. If you're not aware of how you create your story (and we are often not), then there's little chance of you being able to break down the story into 'useful pieces' for the recipient to process. If they can't process it properly, how can they act upon it?

We also often complicate feedback even further by our very human tendency to generalize. Generalization is built into our DNA (figuratively speaking of course). We are learning machines, and we find ways to codify what is learned – especially in our language. Let me explain:

Jean was a manager in an organization. She had come to me because she wanted to explore an issue after challenging her manager for bullying behaviour, and the interaction had not ended well. I asked her what she said to her manager:

JEAN: I told him that he was displaying bullying behaviour and that it was making me feel uncomfortable

CHRIS: So, what happened next?

JEAN: He got very angry and denied it. He was demonstrating the very qualities I was talking about.

CHRIS: So, you actually used the word 'bullying'?

JEAN: Yes.

CHRIS: And what do you mean by the word 'bullying'?

Jean thought about this question and, after quite a bit of thought and reflection, it transpired:

JEAN: I guess he raises his voice and disagrees vehemently with me and then tells me what I 'should' be doing without listening to me.

Notice how difficult it is to communicate all that detail and how much easier it is to use the word 'bullying'. And most of us tend to do this: we use words that have all sorts of meanings packaged up in them. This generalization causes problems because words mean different things to different people, and they have significant experiences attached to them.

When you're not careful with the language you use when giving adjustment feedback, it can cause all kinds of issues. And it's hard to be careful with language when we are not even aware of the story we have constructed. The words we use can be loosely attached to the feelings that we experience, and until we go through a clarification process, our intentions may not always come across clearly.

Effective feedback must take our propensity to generalize into account.

Awareness of feedback situations

Another common problem that crops up is that we are not even aware we are giving feedback, and if that's the case, there's no way to prepare it properly.

For example, I was sitting in on a meeting with a large group of managers and their leadership team – in a forum type setting. One of the leadership team asked what could be done to improve their internal communications. My inner alarm bell started ringing because I've seen these situations before. Improvement questions can often implicitly elicit answers that seem to be critical. One of the junior managers took the bait and went on a tirade about how some processes and communications were causing anger with other managers. I'm sure it was delivered with good intention so things could be improved, but she had not recognized her input could be construed as criticism of someone else's work. She was unknowingly giving someone feedback. As is often my habit, I scanned the room, and I could see one of the senior managers getting more and more irate. Most of the managers then left the room, but the irate manager and another manager remained. The irate manager went on a rant.

> IRATE MANAGER: She's always bloody criticizing. She's so negative. She doesn't understand...
>
> ANOTHER MANAGER: Oh, don't worry about it. She's always negative.

The junior manager had inadvertently stepped into a sensitive feedback situation and hadn't realized it, creating potential foes in the process and damaging her own reputation. If only she had recognized this was the case – she might have chosen a very different way to say it.

I think you'd be surprised by the number of times each day you inadvertently give feedback without realizing it. It happens to me all the time – still. Think about it – disagreements, arguments, corrections and nagging are all forms of adjustment feedback. The other day I counted about 14 times in a single day. And I'm not even good at counting!

Power affects communication

Whether we like it or not, power in organizations distorts the way we communicate; it affects what we think we can say and what we think we cannot.

If you're thinking of giving feedback to someone who you think possesses greater power in the organization, you're probably going to think twice about giving it. You'll also likely experience more emotion at the thought of doing so. These heightened emotions make it tougher to break down and communicate with clarity the feedback you want to give. I've seen highly confident and competent people crumble in conversations with people they perceive as more powerful. They often run out of things to say, and their minds go blank.

But it also works the other way too. If you have more 'organizational or social power' than the person(s), you are delivering the feedback to, they'll more than likely be on high alert, putting your feedback through additional filtering systems. They may be guarded in their response, and the conversation never really develops into one that can help the situation. It's not collaborative and all too often is one way. It makes adjustment feedback feel much more unsafe for everyone.

Safety must, therefore, be considered when power dynamics come into play if adjustment feedback is to be effective.

The power dynamic is often underestimated, and not enough thought is put into what kind of power structures we want to encourage in our organizations. The consequences of these dynamics are not small. Information tends to flow one way, and even then, it can be highly filtered. Leaders need good, accurate information fed back up to them, to make the right decisions.

People are sensitive souls at heart

I think we are all sensitive souls at heart. We want to be loved and accepted for who we are. Most of us want to be liked, and our first reaction to adjustment feedback can be to protect ourselves. We want to reinforce the positive image we have of ourselves. Some people link any feedback to their core identity, so instead of understanding that specific behaviour needs adjusting, they think their core being needs adjusting – a much harder proposition. Because of this, safety needs to be built into the feedback process. We'll explore more about this later in Chapter 8.

We have at least three modes of communication

When we communicate, we don't just communicate with the language we use, but also with our tone of voice and our body language – if you like – three modes of communication. It's not an issue if these modes stay aligned, but when we are in conflict or feeling stressed, these modes of communication are often misaligned. How many times have you disbelieved someone when they said they would do something, but their tones or body language said otherwise? Many arguments happen, not because of what is said, but in the way it is said. I can't recall the number of mini arguments I have with my wife Karen, because of this. She reacts to my tone. I then react to her tone, and the whole thing escalates.

The problem is that our tone and body language tend to be unconscious, and if we don't properly prepare our emotional state before giving feedback, the message we send will be very mixed. That is one reason why we should think doubly hard before giving feedback in a frustrated or angry state.

If we don't prepare our feedback systematically, any inner dilemmas will probably be communicated by the three modes, not playing nicely together.

The heart of the dilemma

All the reasons above bring us to the heart of the dilemma. If you're going to give someone information about them in some way they may not like, will it damage your relationship? Should you give it and risk hurting the relationship or should you stay quiet and suffer in silence. That's the perceived dilemma.

A couple of years ago, there was a situation that illustrated this quite nicely. We live in a row of terraced housing and noticed a noise resembling a washing machine starting in the early hours of the morning: it was rumbly, noisy and annoying. It was also difficult to identify exactly where the noise was emanating. We initially created a story that it was one of our neighbours being insensitive by automatically setting their washing machine to 'on' too early in the morning. We got on quite well with our neighbours but how do we go about broaching this? Do we have the right to even bring it up? What might be early for us might not be early for them. What if they took offence? We might ruin a perfectly good relationship. Was it even them?

It felt easier to just ignore the noise, but the truth was, it was annoying us. What should we do? Sound familiar?

This illustrates the heart of the dilemma, which can often make preparing and delivering feedback much more emotional.

Some people address it by watering down their feedback, which doesn't address the issues at hand. Others try to sandwich their feedback to make the other person feel better, which often leads to mixed messaging. The 'sandwich method' usually goes as follows:

1. Tell them something good about themselves.
2. Tell them the feedback you want to tell them.
3. Finish off by reiterating what is good about them.

This works for some people, but in my programs, a large proportion say they have mixed results. What tends to happen is that people get a mixed message which dilutes the feedback. The result can be a feeling of cynicism toward the giver of feedback.

I remember an old boss of mine giving me feedback using this method.

> BOSS: Hey, Chris, can I give you some feedback?
>
> CHRIS: Yeah, sure.
>
> BOSS: You know, I really think you are very creative in what you do.
>
> CHRIS: [*Thinking: Yeah... and...*]
>
> BOSS: You could have been more proactive in the way you dealt with that issue. I know it wasn't easy, but you could have approached it differently.
>
> CHRIS: [*Thinking: If I could have approached it differently, I would have approached it differently.*]
>
> BOSS: But generally, I'm very pleased with your performance.

Maybe it's just me, but the structure of the communication didn't lend itself naturally to having a useful conversation regarding the issues. The language used encouraged me to have an unnecessary inner dialogue and to second guess his meaning as to what it was exactly, I needed to change and felt like he and I, were avoiding a useful, honest talk.

I believe feedback must be honest and upfront, no game playing, because that can send mixed messages and hurt the relationship. It also needs to be done in such a way as to build up the relationship, not tear it down.

For adjustment feedback to be successful, we must take all the reasons above into account. We must first gain the right to give feedback, build as much trust as possible, agree on a common story and do it in an easy-to-break down fashion. And to do this, we must take the time to prepare our feedback. The preparation doesn't have to be long, and the more we practice it, the quicker we can do it. I believe that even complex feedback can be prepared well in just a few seconds.

Finally, the feedback must be done in a transparent, honest, yet sensitive fashion, because at the end of the day, we need our relationships to remain intact or, even better, to grow. I know that might sound like a lot of criteria just to give a bit of feedback, but the good news is there is a way to do this, and it's not super complex, and we'll begin to explore this in the next chapter.

Recap

- A level of trust is vital for successful Collaborative Feedback. For feedback to achieve its goal, it must be delivered in such a way that the intention is heard
- We are story-making machines. Problems arise when we share our individual stories like they are the truth.
- Giving adjustment feedback is a dance and not a sprint.
- Language, or choice of words, can cause issues. We all tend to package things we have seen or heard into more simplified words or phrases, which others find difficult to unpack.
- Power affects the way feedback is given and received, so it's prudent to be aware of power dynamics.
- We have at least three modes of communication, and these can often be misaligned when we give tricky feedback.
- Be aware of the core dilemma you might be facing – should you give adjustment feedback and risk hurting the relationship or suffer in silence?

CHAPTER 3

ELEMENTS OF SUCCESSFUL COLLABORATIVE FEEDBACK

First, let's start this chapter by talking about what I mean by successful Collaborative Feedback.

Successful Collaborative Feedback is when feedback maximizes the chances of achieving what it sets out to achieve – a useful two-way conversation about the information that is brought up in relation to a goal or outcome.

We can't force people to change the way they think or behave, but we can deliver information in a manner that invites them to really hear and interact with what we have to say. You can't guarantee an outcome, but you can maximize the chances of the information being heard, and you can increase the chances of the conversation being two way. And it's the start of this two-way conversation that leads to better ways of working together.

Typically, these collaborative conversations might end in the recipient of the feedback:

- Seeing the changes, they need to make and go about trying to make them.
- Proposing another perspective and everyone having a different way of seeing things.
- Genuinely hearing the feedback to reflect on it.
- Engaging in a useful coaching type of conversation.

The traits of giving skilled feedback

In running the feedback program over several years, I've noticed patterns, or traits, in people who seem to consistently get a useful two-way interaction with their feedback. They seem to consistently demonstrate these traits when they deliver it. These traits also seem to address the problems we brought up in the previous chapter. For the rest of the chapter we'll explore the elements that seem to encourage successful Collaborative Feedback. People who successfully get others to collaborate during feedback demonstrate the following.

Feedback as a gift

People who tend to get others to collaborate, as a result of feedback conversations, see and treat feedback as a gift and, because of that, deliver it as if it were a gift. They give feedback in a manner that is difficult to reject. They don't necessarily wrap it in cotton wool, because that might lessen the impact of the feedback, but they deliver it in such a way as to invoke curiosity and connection. I personally love gifts because it means the person has thought about me, is offering a gesture of goodwill and wants to make my life that little bit more special.

I look forward to opening it and am at the same time curious and touched. You wouldn't usually force a gift on someone – you offer it. And you'd offer it in a way that communicates it's a gift.

Feedback is a gift. It's a gift that helps you to know if you are on the right path. And I also notice that someone who receives feedback as if it were a gift, is much more likely to utilize the information to improve. Those that don't see feedback as a gift are more likely to reject it.

In one of my workshops, a participant told me about someone they knew who had a reputation for delivering feedback which was never offensive or judgemental – even though a lot of what she said was hard-hitting. I asked what was it that enabled her to come across this way. The answer was that it always seemed to be delivered in a way that it could not be refused. The intention of helpfulness consistently came across loud and clear – even if the content was inherently challenging.

In the following chapter, we'll explore how feedback can be delivered as a gift or a "present" without watering down the content in any way whatsoever.

Preparing feedback

Periodically I'll ask people how they go about giving feedback. I remember one such conversation with a senior manager, which went something like this:

> SENIOR MANAGER: I know when I need to give feedback. I don't need to prepare it. I just go with my gut and shoot from the hip. You've got to be honest, and people see me as an honest guy. What they get is what they see. No messing about. No fluffing it up. No wrapping it up nicely. You must be straight with people.
>
> CHRIS: And how does it usually go?
>
> SENIOR MANAGER: Well, people are often resistant to my input, but at least I've said what I needed to say, and they know where I stand and they know where they stand.

His answer suggested that his feedback often didn't produce the results he was hoping for. And I agree - it is good that everyone knows where he stands and that they think he's straight talking. However, is the goal of feedback just to say what we need to say or is it something more? I think we can do much better.

Let's be honest. The senior manager's style of straight shooting – on the fly, tell-it-as-it-is feedback – works for some people but not others. Some people can get away with it, without causing too many problems, others can't. It's risky. When it works, it's great. When it doesn't, the fallout can be damaging. But I'd guess in his case when it worked, it worked despite how it was delivered.

I've seen many, many examples of managers giving colleagues challenging feedback with no preparation, and it has resulted in unnecessary conflict, hurt, and even tears. There's a saying that goes, 'Sticks and stones will break my bones, but words will never harm me'. Sadly, in organizational life that often doesn't seem to be true.

My experience is, people who give challenging feedback with little or no preparation are playing a risky game. Sometimes it achieves what they want it to achieve. Often it does not and causes problems with those who receive it.

Another thing I notice is that people who give challenging feedback are processing the information as they talk; they're operating on the fly. This runs the risk of the recipient misunderstanding the intention of what they are saying – especially if they, are working out their intention as they speak. It can lead to significant misunderstandings and result in no collaboration whatsoever. There are of course exceptions to the rule. One of these seems to be the quality of the relationship between the giver of feedback and recipient. Relationships with high levels of trust seem to get past the words – to the deeper intent.

There have been several occasions in my career where I've decided to give potentially challenging feedback without preparation – on the spur of the moment - shoot from the hip if you will. Nearly always, I've felt bad afterwards, hoping that I hadn't said the wrong thing. Sometimes I got away with it, but often I was left having to work hard to repair the relationship. And on a few occasions, I ruined the relationship. Many participants on my programs report something similar if they are asked the question – especially those that particularly value relationships.

Wilhelm shot from the hip and caused carnage.

Feedback tends to land much better when we take time to clear our thinking and work through what we want to achieve and what we want to say. To do this, we may have to work through conflicts in our minds. The problem is when you get sensitive situations, where you feel like you need to say something, processing the information feels difficult. And this is where a simple structure (at least initially) can really help you prepare your feedback – efficiently, effectively, authentically – to encourage a two-way conversation. This is also one of the goals of this book: to provide you with a robust structure to prepare the feedback you want to give.

I've found, most people are much more confident when they take the time and effort to process what they are going to say – especially if the feedback is potentially delicate. And let's be honest, you can never really know if the feedback you give will touch some sensitive spots, so why not prepare it anyway?

Get into the habit of preparing your feedback. With a little bit of practice, you will be able to thoroughly prepare it efficiently – in real time. Then, you can deliver it confidently and congruently, knowing it's likely to achieve what it sets out to.

Recognizing feedback situations as they arise

Being great at collaboration means tuning into feedback situations as they appear. Why is this important? Because we regularly get feedback situations within feedback situations and the nature of the feedback can change mid-conversation. A typical example is when you have a conversation about a topic with a colleague, and you get the feeling, from what they say, they don't understand what you're attempting to communicate. The conversation then has to temporarily change to address that issue, before you can progress with the original topic.

A few years ago, I witnessed a piece of feedback given by one member of staff to another, which clearly demonstrates this in action:

COLLEAGUE A: Can I give you a bit of feedback about the team meeting?

COLLEAGUE B: Yeah, sure.

COLLEAGUE A: You could have spoken with a bit more energy.

COLLEAGUE B: [*Eyes glazing over.*] Alright. Thanks.

There were a few moments of silence before Colleague A continued.

COLLEAGUE A: You seem a bit defensive.

COLLEAGUE B: I'm not at all... and I don't appreciate you saying that.

COLLEAGUE A: I'm sorry. I didn't mean to offend.

COLLEAGUE B: [*Silence.*]

Initially, the feedback from Colleague A was about Colleague B's lack of energy in the meeting. Halfway through this short interchange, the topic switched from being lacklustre to being defensive – this is what I mean by feedback within feedback. If you're unaware of when and how new feedback situations arise, you may find the conversation ending awkwardly – as did this example.

Feedback situations occur more often than you think. Even after running feedback programs for several years, I'm often surprised when I discover that I've actually been in an adjustment feedback conversation that I didn't realize was a feedback conversation. This happens both at work and at home. If you've ever had a heated argument and think back on the conversation, I'll bet that just before the argument erupted, some form of feedback was given. And I'll bet one party wasn't aware of it.

Consider this: anytime you engage in a conversation where you request someone to change direction in their thinking or behaviour (implicitly or explicitly) – you are in a feedback situation. That means any debate or argument is implicitly a feedback conversation. In a debate or dispute, you are giving others feedback on their thinking. And this is why a conversation in a bar can often spiral into a raging argument. If you are unable to recognize you are in a feedback situation, you can't treat it like a feedback situation – and you can't prepare it as such.

I encountered one such scenario the other night that I think you might be familiar with. My wife had just kindly taken time to prepare a lovely pasta dish for myself and our two children. If you know my wife, you'll know she doesn't like cooking, nor does she think she's good at it, it's more like a labour of love for her. On this occasion, it was her turn to cook, (as if to imply that we take equal turns – let me be clear – we do not – she's much more equal than me) and she had made great efforts to try and create a new dish. A few minutes after serving the meal, a conversation started:

KAREN: How's the meal?

CHRIS: Great… although it could do with a bit more salt.

KAREN: [*Pause.*] Well, maybe next time you cook a meal, you can make sure that you can personally add it yourself

CHRIS: I wasn't criticizing your cooking.

KAREN: I'm sure you think you weren't. But you were!

How did I put myself in that hole? Only by not recognizing it was a feedback situation. Some of you may be thinking, 'Are you advocating that we not be honest as to what we truly think?' or 'Are you advocating that we tread on tenterhooks about what we should say?' No and no. I'm merely saying be aware of feedback situations and be mindful of the ramifications.

When we are aware of the layers of feedback that lie within any conversation, we can adapt and apply the principles that make for good feedback, to preserve and enhance all our relationships.

Being mindful of intention

People who tend to be successful in their feedback conversations are highly aware of their intentions when they deliver feedback.

In a high-stakes conversation, our intentions can change in an instant. I remember having a feedback conversation with my son a few years ago – something to do with helping him revise for his exams. It started well, but then he said something that offended me – I can't even remember what it was – something about his tone and what he said. My intention changed from trying to help him revise better, to putting him back in his place for being disrespectful. I didn't do it purposely. It just switched. The conversation changed course and became much less useful. I dare say it ended badly.

I see this often happening in the workplace too. A coaching conversation can swiftly transform to a 'my way is better' conversation. A boardroom exploration can soon turn into a 'who's right and who's wrong' conversation.

The intention is crucial because it drives our behaviours subconsciously. Our intentions influence the way we feel, and the way we feel, influences how we communicate. Intention can, therefore, support or derail our conversations.

Sometimes we hold several intentions at the same time, and these can work against one another. We want to vent our frustration and be helpful at the same time; we want to lash out yet want to be respectful in the same instant. At the very least, if we are not mindful of our different intentions, we can send out mixed messaging which will impact on the collaboration we are searching for.

As I mentioned in a previous chapter, as humans, we are emotional beings. A participant on one of my programs told me about a situation that had happened at her workplace. She was a consultant for a large firm, and they had been working on an important project for a client over a prolonged period. The team had worked long hours through challenging circumstances. One day their client expressed concerns to the project leader. The leader felt frustrated and gathered the whole project team together for a meeting, which ended in several of the team feeling discouraged and demotivated – and some saying they no longer wished to work for the business.

I had a coaching conversation with the project lead, and part of our conversation went something like this:

CHRIS: So, that I can understand more clearly the nature of the interaction, what exactly did you say to the team?

PROJECT LEAD: I told them that as a team we were rubbish and if we didn't pull our socks up, we would lose the contract.

CHRIS: Definitely straight talking. Were those your actual words? Did you use the word 'rubbish'?

PROJECT LEAD: As far as I can recall, yes.

CHRIS: And can I ask, what was your intention in saying that?

PROJECT LEAD: I wanted them to change – perform better.

CHRIS: Was there anything else that made you choose the word 'rubbish'?

PROJECT LEAD: I don't think so. Well, I guess I was frustrated. The project's crucial to me. The results of it will impact my career.

CHRIS: Now that you've had some time to reflect, would you have done it the same way?

PROJECT LEAD: Probably not. I would have chosen different words and perhaps not gotten the whole group together… I guess I was frustrated.

It became apparent that the project lead had mixed intentions. Partly he wanted to help his team change their performance, but he also wanted to vent how frustrated he was. This is not an uncommon scenario and can swiftly sabotage any collaboration that could come from a feedback conversation.

Sometimes, we don't know how we feel, but we subconsciously act according to our intentions. I can't tell you the number of times I've given feedback to my children believing that I am helping them to develop, but later in hindsight realized that I was expressing my anger or frustration at something they'd done. And do they pick that up? You bet. And then they react, and the conversation goes off course.

In a professional environment, your colleagues might not react, but the result is the same: the conversation is derailed. This is why it's vital you have an awareness of what emotional state you are in and what intentions you are holding.

Being mindful of outcomes

An outcome is what you want to happen as a result of the conversation. People who successfully get others to collaborate from a feedback conversation are also mindful of the outcome. They find a way to successfully hold the outcome as the frame for the conversation. They do this by making the outcome explicit or find some skilful way to express it implicitly. If they feel the outcome frame is lost during the conversation, they bring it back, so that everyone is clear where the conversation is heading.

When you take time to clarify your outcome in giving feedback, you can often gain insights about your intentions because sometimes they can be different from what you think they are. Once you've got clarity on your outcome, you can think about how to best achieve it. Sometimes the clarity will tell you that your outcome is inappropriate and inform you whether you should even embark upon the feedback conversation. A colleague of mine was considering giving feedback to another colleague after an event that hadn't gone according to plan. We had a conversation that went something like this:

CHRIS: What outcome do you want as a result of having this conversation?

COLLEAGUE: That he changes his behaviour.

CHRIS: So, you want him to be more considerate of your time?

COLLEAGUE: Not just that – I also want him to know how annoying he can be.

CHRIS: So, you also want him to know that he can be annoying?

COLLEAGUE: Sounds like I'm just having a go at him, doesn't it?

CHRIS: A little.

My colleague decided not to have that conversation at that time – methinks a wise choice. Because when feedback givers don't or can't effectively communicate the purpose and outcome of their feedback, it can easily lead to misunderstanding, stress or confusion. Think about the following questions:

- How many times have you wondered where a feedback conversation is going? What exactly are they trying to say? Why do they seem hesitant? And what are they implying?
- How many times have you started a feedback conversation and it's gone down a different path to the one you intended?
- How many times have you forgotten what you wanted to say in the first place with the feedback?
- How many times has the recipient of feedback accused you of 'having a go', when all you were trying to do was help?

If the outcome remains undeclared, your intentions, as the giver of feedback, can easily be misconstrued. To find the outcome ask a simple question:

What do I want to happen as a result of the feedback I give?

When we ask this question, we gain insight as to our true intention, which then helps us to moderate our own behaviours as to when and how we give feedback.

Another common issue that crops up is this: people who give feedback sometimes hold outcomes that are either unrealistic or unreasonable. This causes problems because it means the receiver of feedback is unlikely to collaborate. Sometimes the outcomes we want are too much of a stretch to the person to whom we are giving the feedback. They can't do it even if they want to. Or they won't do it because it's so far from their thinking. In cases like these, finding an alternative intermediary outcome could be more useful. Let me explain with the following example.

Jane was a manager in one of my programs and the mother of a teenage daughter. She was getting annoyed because her daughter had the habit of rolling her eyes at her when in serious conversation. As part of the program, she gave feedback to her daughter on this issue and fed back the result of her conversation:

> JANE: I wish you'd stop rolling your eyes at me. It's disrespectful.
>
> DAUGHTER: I wish a lot of things too.

The conversation then went downhill, so I had a conversation with Jane to ask about her intended outcome.

> CHRIS: What outcome were you holding when you gave the feedback?
>
> JANE: I want her to stop rolling her eyes at me because it's disrespectful.
>
> CHRIS: Have you ever told her that before?

JANE: Yes, lots of times.

CHRIS: And has she changed that behaviour?

JANE: Well, no.

CHRIS: What if you held a different outcome when you give feedback?

JANE: What do you mean?

CHRIS: What if your outcome was to understand 'why' she was rolling her eyes, instead of expecting her to stop doing it?

JANE: Would that make a difference?

CHRIS: Try it and see.

Jane then went back and had a different feedback conversation with her daughter, which went something like this:

JANE: I notice that your eyes roll upward when we talk about certain subjects. Am I saying something wrong?

DAUGHTER: No, it's just that you say things I already know. And if I could change it, I would.

The discussion became a fruitful one, which led to more understanding on both sides, and Jane relayed how much closer she felt to her daughter as a result.

Holding a different outcome changes how you approach a feedback conversation. Often the key to a fruitful feedback conversation is finding an outcome that is likely to be agreeable to both sides. It's a kind of negotiation. Sometimes it's better to have a series of feedback conversations that lead to the ultimate outcome you want, rather than trying to do it all in one go.

Another thing that can happen with outcomes is that sometimes your intention– and with it, the outcome – will change midway during a conversation. This happened to me the other day with my son.

CHRIS: Can I remind you that you promised to take your stuff out of the living room and into your room?

SON: I was just about to do it.

CHRIS: No, you weren't, you were sitting up there playing video games.

SON: No, I wasn't.

CHRIS: Yes, you were.

SON: No, I wasn't. Do you have x-ray eyes or something? You were downstairs in your office, and I was upstairs – so how would you know?

Do you see what subtly happened in that exchange? I was giving feedback to get a change in my son's behaviour. Half-way through the conversation, my intention and outcome changed – the goal became more about being right. Be aware when the goal of your conversation shifts because it muddies the communication, and you may find yourself going down a different route; different than you intended.

Giving feedback when you are angry or frustrated simply doesn't work. People pick up emotions subconsciously, and warning signals begin to fire – which takes them away from the conversation you are trying to have. And this leads us nicely to the next point.

Keeping eyes and ears open

People who consistently get others to have collaborative

conversations tend to be aware of how the recipient is responding to the feedback in real time. They observe the other person as they give feedback. They keep their eyes and ears open so they can see how the person is responding. They do this because they recognize feedback is a dance. If you're not aware of what's changing in a dance situation, you'll invariably step on toes. As a result, they don't only focus on the content of what they are discussing. They focus intently on the other person. They scan to see how the other person is reacting. And because they also see feedback as a gift, they adjust how the gift is delivered.

Creating an environment of safety

Creating an atmosphere of safety is critical for adjustment feedback. We talked in the previous chapter about how some people can take feedback personally, how language is open to interpretation, and how assumptions are so easy to make – and these can all result in social judgement. Most people hate being judged; they react to assumptions and put up resistance to predetermined outcomes. All these things can cause the recipient to feel threatened.

It's well-documented that when people feel socially threatened, it activates their flight, fight or freeze mechanism. When in danger, animals' defence systems kick in. Sometimes they fight back, sometimes they run from danger, and sometimes they keep very still, hoping that the predator doesn't notice them and eventually go away. Evolutionary psychology informs us that humans have developed these mechanisms to fight enemies, run from dangerous situations or freeze to hide from a predator. Unfortunately, the amygdala (the part of our brain that senses danger) sometimes misinterprets danger in social situations and sets off a false alarm. The body then enters survival mode quicker than the rational mind can react, and we may feel in real mortal danger, even though we aren't.

In survival mode, we tend to engage in protective behaviours, which don't tend to result in collaborative conversations!

People who successfully invite others to collaborate are aware of this natural response and make efforts to help the recipient feel safe. They find ways to minimize judgement and anything else that causes social threat. They pay attention to the physical environment and what's around them. They seem to lay out their thinking for others to see – so that others can explore it as objectively as possible. They initially come across as less sure and more curious. They stay away from stories of blame and finger-pointing. They also reduce the uncertainty of the situation. We'll specifically talk about how to do this later.

Being aware of your state

It's natural to be nervous when we think we are criticizing others. It's also natural for us to react when we think we are being criticized. In these situations, stress levels can rise and can come out in an inappropriate expression of vocal tone and body language. When arguments over silly things occur, often they are driven by the tone and body language that are present during the conversation. And it's our state that drives tone and nonverbal expressions. It might go something like this. I notice your raised eyebrows. I think you are questioning me. I raise my tone and volume. You pick up on my tone and volume and increase yours. I pick up on that and react. Very soon it begins to escalate, and we find ourselves in a shouting match. That's why we must be mindful of our states.

Unless you are aware of your state – how you are feeling and how you are communicating – you have very little chance of modifying your tone and nonverbal communication leading to unnecessary escalation and therefore lack of safety.

Those that get great collaboration are aware of what's happening internally as they deliver the feedback.

Breaking down information in to see/hear data

Those that promote Collaborative Feedback make it as easy as possible for the recipient to use the information they're given. In adjustment feedback, language can be a problem. As human beings, we tend to code what we see into language labels that simply aren't useful to those who hear it. Words like 'lazy', 'inefficient', 'sensible', 'confident' (and hundreds of other commonly used words) are all labels for sequences of behaviours and events, which are often complex in nature. These language labels communicate judgement instead of help and are notoriously difficult to break down.

A few years ago, I was talking to a manager who worked for an investment bank, and he shared how a feedback conversation with one of his staff hadn't gone as well as expected.

CHRIS: What did you say to him?

MANAGER: I fed back to him that he was disrespectful in the interaction.

CHRIS: And what specifically did you mean by 'disrespectful'?

MANAGER: Well, you know... disrespectful. He just was.

CHRIS: OK, let me ask it another way. How specifically did you know he was disrespectful? What did you see or hear specifically?

MANAGER: Ummmm... I'm not sure exactly.

After further questioning, it transpired that what the manager meant by 'disrespectful' was:

- The tone of the staff member wasn't quite right.
- The staff member wasn't looking at the manager in the 'right' way when they were conversing.
- The staff member used 'certain words' that the manager didn't like in that situation.
- Halfway through the conversation, the staff member had turned his body, as if getting ready to leave, even though the manager had not finished speaking.

After this information came out, I asked the manager what he thought about our conversation, and he said, 'Wow, I never realized that was what I was thinking and what I really meant by 'disrespectful'. There's no way, he would ever have got that from the words I used in my feedback to him. Even more than that, I'm not sure I would have embarked on this particular conversation.'

Breaking these labels down into bite-sized chunks that communicate what you specifically saw and heard will make your feedback much more useful. Even more powerful (as you can see from the example above), as you break down these labels, you'll begin to see if you have the clarity to give that specific feedback and if what you are saying makes sense. Once again, we see the huge need to prepare our feedback before we give it.

Believing feedback is part of a co-creation process

People who elicit collaborative responses often have a belief that adjustment feedback is a co-creative experience. They believe they have a perspective that might help shape the perspective of others. They share their experience and make explicit their beliefs of cause and effect. It's a bit like saying, 'I may have parts of a better picture. You have parts of it too. Let's join up and form this thing!'

It's helpful to communicate the implications of the information you are sharing. Why is being late detrimental to the workplace? How does not being energetic in a presentation affect its impact on the audience? Why is neglecting networking a bad thing? Why can't I say what I just said in the board meeting? People might not connect the feedback given to the situation at hand. As a result, they wonder why the information has been offered at all.

Sometimes people just haven't had the same types of experience as you. They don't know what you are talking about or why, and they are unlikely to make the right connections. In other words, feedback conversations are a blending of perspectives, and if you think of it this way, you are much more likely to get collaboration.

Making sure it's a two-way conversation

You want to make sure the person to whom you give feedback has heard it. You also want to make sure, as much as possible, they aren't creating some wild story that isn't connected to your initial intention in giving it. And you'd be surprised by the stories that rational people make up – even in the workplace.

I want to reiterate - you can't force someone to change, but you can at least make every effort to ensure that the information is heard in the way it's supposed to be heard. That's why two-way communication is imperative.

It's good practice to think of communication as being two way – always; it's a loop, and it's not completed until you know what you've said has been heard – the right way. When you tell someone something, you need to have some sort of mechanism to find out whether the listener has heard you and whether the listener has heard you right.

The success of adjustment feedback being a two-way conversation is mostly dependent on how well you follow the principles above: how you build safety, how clear and acceptable your intentions and outcomes are, and ultimately what kind of an interaction you want to have with the recipient of the feedback.

In the next chapter, we'll start exploring what I call the 'PRESENT Model of Collaborative Feedback', which puts these principles into practice.

Recap

- Think of feedback as a gift – both when giving it and receiving it.
- Take time to prepare your feedback because you know it may be more complex than you first thought.
- Be acutely aware of when feedback situations arise.
- Be aware of your intentions and be mindful that you may have more than one.
- Be clear about the intended outcome of the feedback conversation and always keep it in mind .
- Keep your eyes and ears open to see how the other person is reacting and adjust accordingly – recognize it's a dance.
- Create environments of safety.
- Break down information into things you can actually see and actually hear.
- Make feedback a two-way conversation.

CHAPTER 4

THE PRESENT MODEL OF COLLABORATIVE FEEDBACK

We've already explored how feedback is a gift and the traits that are likely to result in collaboration. When we combine these two concepts, we have what I think is a robust model of feedback, which I call the 'PRESENT Model of Collaborative Feedback'. It's nice to give and receive presents, and at Curious Learning, we want people everywhere, in organizations, to take on this mindset. When you give feedback, think of it as a present. It'll make it a lot easier to give it and you'll find people are much more likely to take it. When on the receiving end of feedback, think of it also as a present. When you get to unwrap it, it will contain some pleasant surprises that will help you later in your life.

The PRESENT Model is about how to *start* a feedback conversation so that it continues in a useful exchange that benefits both parties. It's not about getting the recipient of the feedback to change. Achieving change is more about the effectiveness of your coaching and ability to influence, which is beyond the scope of this book. There are plenty of books written on those topics.

Seven steps

So, after all the preamble, here is the PRESENT Model of Collaborative Feedback:

1. **P**repare feedback.
2. **R**evisit outcome

3. **E**motional State.
4. **S**ee/hear behaviours
5. **E**xpose thinking
6. **N**arrative is only ever mine
7. **T**wo-way conversation

Here's how the PRESENT Model links to the traits we explored in the previous chapter. Look at the diagram below:

THE 'PRESENT' MODEL OF COLLABORATIVE FEEDBACK	ELEMENTS OF SUCCESSFUL COLLABORATIVE FEEDBACK
PREPARE FEEDBACK	They prepare feedback They recognize feedback situations as they arise They create an environment of safety
REVISIT OUTCOME	They are mindful of intention They are mindful of their outcomes
EMOTIONAL STATE	They are aware of their state They create an environment of safety
SEE / HEAR BEHAVIOURS	They break down information into see / hear data They create an environment of safety
EXPOSE THINKING	They see feedback as a gift They create an environment of safety They believe feedback is part of a co-creative process
NARRATIVE IS ONLY EVER MINE	They create an environment of safety
TWO-WAY CONVERSATION	They make sure it's a two-way conversation They keep their eyes and ears open They believe feedback is part of a co-creative process

The PRESENT Model accounts for all 14 of the traits we identified in the previous chapter. It takes care to build safety for the recipient, takes pre-emptive action against potential barriers and works to calm the survival instinct in the brain. It makes it easier for the recipient to process the feedback usefully. Essentially, it allows you to compellingly lay your thinking on the table and extends an invitation for all to explore together.

In the rest of the chapter, we'll look at how to go about applying these steps and give a few examples of how it's done.

1. Prepare feedback

When you recognize a situation in which feedback is required, you must first process your thinking before giving feedback. This is necessary because feedback situations are often not clear cut. There are often conflicts that exist in our minds that can muddy how we deliver it.

We won't spend too long on preparation right now, because the next chapter is devoted to that very topic. All I'll say is preparation needs to be quick, easy and comprehensive. Otherwise, most people just won't get round to doing it. It almost needs to be done in real time as opportunities arise.

At Curious Learning, we've developed a tool that will do just that. It's a simple way of preparing feedback via several sentence starters and doesn't take long to learn. In our training courses, most people memorize it quickly. Getting into the habit of rapidly preparing your feedback is a must for successful adjustment feedback.

2. Revisit outcome

This is a critical step if the feedback is to end in a collaboration. The outcome you choose must be appropriate and realistic – and, at some point during the conversation, both the giver and receiver must have a common understanding and agreement of it, if it is to end collaboratively. The outcome informs the context which is critical in ensuring the feedback gets across in the right way. If you don't set the context adequately, you're playing dice with how the recipient can interpret the feedback. Therefore, both the outcome and context must be clearly communicated. Otherwise, the conversation has higher chances of ending in resistance. Let's explore why getting the outcome right is important.

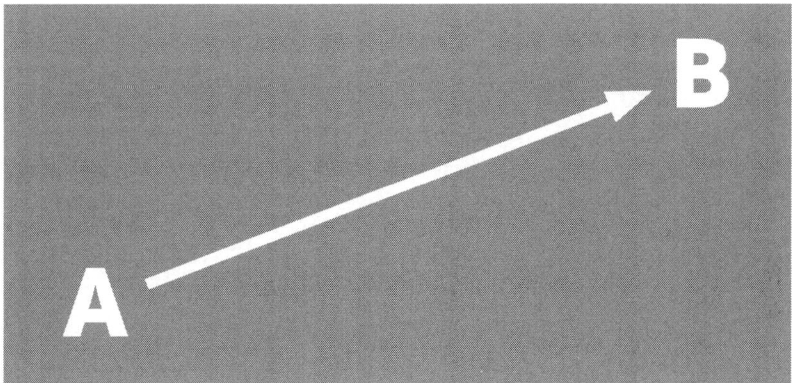

Look at the simple diagram above. Let's imagine taking a journey from point A to B. Point A is where we are now. Point B is where we want to get to. Examples of point B might be:

- Ensuring we perform a task to the right standard.
- Ensuring that the steps of a process are done in the right order.

- Ensuring we execute the steps of a sales model effectively.
- Having a reputation for getting things done.
- Being more efficient in using spreadsheets.
- Having a good understanding of the political environment inside the workplace.
- Ensuring the elements of a proposal are easy to understand and compelling.
- Ensuring the objectives of a meeting are fulfilled within the time allowed.
- Meeting an essential key performance indicator (KPI).
- Increasing our personal network.

You can probably think of thousands more if you tried. If point B is where we want to get to, then feedback (both adjustment and affirmational) is information as to where we are in our journey and how we are doing in getting there. That's all feedback ever is. (Notice that point B doesn't even have to be a definitive, measurable point. In the case of 'increasing your personal network', point B is simply an upward trend.) Affirmational feedback is simply 'you're doing great in your journey keep going'. Adjustment feedback is 'You might want to look at how you're doing – you seem to be going off course,' or 'You might be able to get there a bit faster.' This is the fundamental structure of any type of personal feedback.

But let's focus on point B a little more closely. Sometimes in giving feedback, we inadvertently create a point B that has never been the recipient's point B due to our story creation mechanisms. Or, alternatively, we create a point B that's inappropriate because point B isn't within the person's reach; they feel incapable of getting there.

Let me give you an example. Katy was an ambitious operations director in a large organization. Keith was one of her direct reports. Katy had very high hopes for Keith, who she regarded as 'extremely talented'. The business was going through tough times, and the senior management team had identified some activities they thought would turn things around. Tension had developed between the two because Katy was putting in longer and longer hours, staying late and had expectations that others should do the same. Keith frequently left the office at around 6 p.m. During a half-yearly appraisal, Katy gave Keith some feedback, and it went something like this:

> KATY: I'm disappointed that you're not showing the commitment that others are – in turning the business around. It's vital that everyone pulls their weight. Especially you, because you are so talented.
>
> KEITH: I beg to disagree. I am committed to the business.

The conversation went downhill from there. A few months later, Keith found another job and left the business. Katy was left with a big hole in her team, leaving her feeling even more disappointed.

If Katy had prepared her feedback, she might have realized that the outcome she held was different from Keith's. Hers was something like – there is a standard of commitment right now, and you are falling short of it. You need to adjust your behaviour so it falls in line with the standard. What she failed to realize was that he had never agreed to that standard of commitment and so they were embarking on the wrong conversation. It's a bit like holding someone accountable to a goal they've never agreed to – it doesn't work. It's sensible to first check that you share a common outcome.

Sometimes you have to focus on an intermediary outcome to get to the feedback conversation you really want to have. You must build the bridge close enough to give you a chance of jumping and landing on the other side. Giving feedback on something that no one has really agreed to, is going to end in unnecessary conflict – whether overt or passive.

The 'outcome' and 'why it's important' also needs to be clearly communicated. Do they even know that the conversation is about point B? A common thing I notice is that people ascribe the wrong context to the conversation and, because they are talking from different frames of reference in the first place, the conversation has little chance of ending well. All too often the recipient is simply confused about why the feedback has been given.

An example of this was given by one of my program participants, Ayesha, during the embedding of her feedback training. She revealed it was a pattern of conversation that had repeated consistently over several years. Ayesha had a son, and they had been arguing about household chores for several years. She relayed a typical conversation to me:

AYESHA: Your room is disgusting.

SON: Why are you having a go at me?

AYESHA: I'm not having a go at you.

SON: Yes, you are.

AYESHA: No, I'm not.

SON: Yes, you are.

This would then quickly descend into an argument which ended with one of them stomping off.

Ayesha and I had a conversation about how to change this pattern into something more useful. I suggested she focused a little more precisely on the context and outcome of her opening gambit. Ayesha made the context clearer, and the results were different. This is how the updated version of the feedback went.

AYESHA: Can we chat about our agreement regarding the tidiness of your room? I notice there are lots of objects lying on the floor and lots of cups on your table.

SON: Erm… It's not very good, is it? I'll get around to doing it.

AYESHA: Could you do it soon, please?

SON: OK.

Did it guarantee Ayesha's son would tidy up? Who knows – only Ayesha and her son, but the conversation went much better, and Ayesha was able to have much better success when she gave feedback in this way.

Notice the subtle change in context. In the first example, point B wasn't made explicit. In the absence of point B, Ayesha's son seemed to be making one up – in this case, it was, 'You don't think I'm good enough.' In the second example, point B is made explicit. The option of inventing an alternative point B is removed, and the conversation went much better. This little change in making point B explicit seemed to make a big difference.

This type of pattern also happens with new starters in organizations as they try and get a feel of how they are doing. This is how the conversation might go:

NEW STARTER: How am I doing?

MANAGER: Great. Just keep going.

The new starter might feel a bit more reassured as to how she's doing, but she's none the wiser as to the specifics. How much more useful would it be if the manager defined the different areas (point B), so the feedback was more specific.

I'm not saying you must *always* state the outcome because sometimes it's obvious, but in the event of feedback going down an unplanned route, check it is clear to everyone.

When you make effort to identify the outcome, it will shed light on some of your own intentions in giving the feedback. Having an appropriate and realistic outcome also helps in building safety. It provides the recipient with some certainty about what the conversation is about and what it's not.

3. Emotional state

You can say the right things in an adjustment feedback conversation, but if there is a hint of anger, frustration or mixed emotion for something the recipient has done or said, you can be sure they will pick it up. Our emotional state drives our behaviours and affects how we communicate. In other words, if you're agitated or frustrated, it will more than likely come out via your vocal tones and body language. And be assured, the recipient will pick it up, even if only at a subconscious level. This makes the conversation feel unsafe for them, their survival instincts will kick in, and they will more than likely engage in defensive behaviours. At the very least, you will be sending a mixed message. It's a sure way to shake the trust in a relationship – and trust is essential. Once trust deteriorates, every conversation becomes hard work.

Wait until your mood has changed and then give feedback. And if it's not appropriate to wait, do your very best to watch your vocal tone, facial expression and body language.

Jack didn't manage his state, and subsequently, his feedback lacked impact.

4. See/hear behaviours

This is very important. Your ability to break down your own stories is an essential part of giving skilful feedback. When we give feedback, we process what we have observed, usually very quickly, and rapidly come to judgements based upon our own criteria and standards. We then package this up into internal language like:

- He's inefficient.

- He isn't very effective.
- She lacks confidence.
- He's often angry.
- He's got an authoritarian management style.
- She micromanages me.
- He's great.
- She's very intuitive.
- She's a great salesperson.

We then give feedback based on these packaged assumptions. It's not necessarily disastrous if you give examples to back up the judgement, but it does bring problems. Here's an example I was privy to hearing. Amir was giving a presentation to the executive team and sought feedback from his manager, the HR Director, afterwards.

> HR DIRECTOR: Your presentation lacked a bit of passion.
>
> AMIR: Oh...
>
> HR DIRECTOR: At times, it was like watching paint dry.
>
> AMIR: Right... erm... OK.
>
> HR DIRECTOR: Next time you need to put a bit more time into preparing it.
>
> AMIR: OK.

There was an awkward silence, and then they both went their separate ways.

Later, Amir confided that he had felt really discouraged by the feedback as he had tried his hardest to deliver a powerful presentation. I asked him what he made of the feedback, and he confessed he didn't really know what to do with it. The feedback didn't help him in any way except to inform him that he lacked passion. That's because the language we are familiar with is well packaged and insulated.

There's a phrase I hear commonly used by parents all over the world to their children… 'You need to change your attitude!' There I've said it.

How many children change their attitude when they hear their parents say this? I'll wager not very many. I always ask the following question in my workshops: 'How many of you have ever had someone say to you "You need to change your attitude?" The vast majority of those present raise their hands.

My next question is: 'How many of you actually changed your attitude when this was said to you?' Not one hand has ever gone up in the many years I have asked this question.

'Attitude' means very little to most people. They simply don't know what to do with it except, of course, sulk and get more attitude-ee!

When we use language like this in our feedback without explaining what we mean by it, it puts the burden on the recipient to unpack it, and lots of people are not skilled enough to do it. They are then left with a label that doesn't help them and feel judged.

Get into the habit of unpacking your language before you give feedback. It's trickier than you think because we are not used to doing it. It'll take a little bit of practice.

To unpack a label, ask yourself one of the following questions:

- What did I specifically ***see*** or ***hear*** that led me to that conclusion?
- What is it you actually ***saw*** and ***heard*** that led you to your judgements?

And it must be specific. You can't see 'attitude'. But you can see a frown. You can't hear 'dispassionate', but you can hear a low volume as someone speaks or hear the pace is slower. You can't see 'reliable', but you can hear they made three promises on various days and they kept them all. If you can't visualize it or replay the dialogue internally, then it's not what you saw or heard. Below are some common feedback words with some possible breakdowns:

- Change your **attitude**: You spoke in monosyllables. There was little eye contact. You looked at the floor most of the time. The tones in which you spoke were very low.
- You need to be more **accountable**: You use phrases like 'he didn't...' 'she didn't...' 'they didn't...' instead of communicating what part you played in the problem.
- You came across as **frustrated**: Your tone was different than usual. You spoke much quicker than you usually would and interrupted me several times mid-sentence.
- You need to be more **strategic**: You made your point without any reference to other contributory factors involved.

- You need to be more **proactive**: You do what you are asked to do, but I don't see you come up with suggestions if you are not asked. You don't do things without someone telling you specifically what to do

So, in summary, when you are breaking down language into see/hear behaviours ask yourself:

- What did I actually hear?
- What did I actually see?

Here's an example from another participant on one of my programs, who went through the process of breaking down language into see/hear behaviours. Elaine was a senior manager in a large public organization. She had noticed an interaction between one of her managers and another staff member which alarmed her because the phrase that sprung to mind was, 'he's bullying her'. Elaine felt a bit concerned about immediately addressing it because, a few years back, she'd had a similar situation, which she'd addressed, but which ended badly. On that occasion, she had used the word 'bullying'. I asked her to break down the word into see/hear language and use the results as part of her feedback.

Here's what she said:

> ELAINE: I noticed an interaction the other day by the coffee machine. You were talking to X about the report. I couldn't help but notice as you were talking that your volume got louder and louder and your facial expressions became more intense. Also, when she tried to say something, you seemed to interrupt her several times. I also noticed that she had a scared look on her face. Now I'm

sure I don't know the whole story, but I would guess that interaction might be intimidating for her and it doesn't seem to fit in with the way we should be managing around here. What do you think?

MANAGER: Oh, wow. I didn't realize I was doing that

The rest of the conversation went well. Elaine was elated.

A side benefit of breaking down language into see/hear behaviours is that as you do so, you will be examining the construction of your own story. This raises awareness of the often-hidden elements that make up the standards and values you hold and gives you insights into how you create your stories.

5. Expose thinking

Lay your thinking on the table for all to see by connecting what you've seen and heard to the meaning you make of that information. You can also articulate consequences and implications to that meaning if appropriate.

When you start an adjustment feedback conversation, quite often the other person will be asking themselves, 'Where is this going and why are we having it?' Providing 'the why' will hugely help the conversation. There are several benefits in relaying the meaning you have attached to your observations:

- It provides clarity as to the reason why you are having the conversation.
- It allows them to gain insight into how you have constructed the story and enables them to process the information usefully.

- It signals unconsciously that you have thought through your feedback.
- It lays bare your thinking for both to examine, which helps build trust and conveys openness and transparency. Doing this will also make you more approachable.

In my programs, I strongly emphasize the principle 'laying bare your thinking for all to examine'. When you do this, it enables the other person to see exactly how you're constructing your story. It's powerful because they gain insight into where you're coming from. Also doing this somehow depersonalizes the situation. It immediately becomes more analytical – more about the information and not so much about them. Laying your thinking on the table also communicates confidence and competence. Only people who are confident and authentic can lay out their thinking for everyone to see.

Implications

As I briefly described, sometimes it's helpful to communicate the implications or consequences of your observations – if they're not already obvious. Why does the lack of strategic thinking mean it's a bad thing? Why is not spending time building your own network bad? What are the implications of handing the report in late? If they're more inexperienced than you, they might not know some of the consequences of their behaviour. One example of this was James, a new addition to senior management. Kevin was his CEO and mentor. Kevin gave some feedback to James after a board meeting: 'I noticed in the board meeting that you spent significant time with Chairman Bob, Greig and Katharine, but not much time connecting with Scott. Scott has enormous influence, and if you don't develop your relationship with him, you'll have little chance of getting decisions through. What do you think?'

Implications can be both natural and artificial and positive or negative. Natural implications are those which naturally occur because of social, business and system dynamics.

For example:

- If you don't plan your work, you are more likely to produce lower quality work.
- If you don't build a relationship with that person, it will be harder to influence them.
- If you don't take culture into account, change initiatives will more than likely fail.
- If you don't pay attention to marketing and sales, your pipeline will dry up.
- If you shout at your brother, expect conflict.
- If you keep driving people without regard for welfare, they may burn out.
- Taking care of your own welfare will lead to you being more resourceful.
- Understanding the organization's systems will enable you to solve problems quicker.
- Doing useful things without being asked will enhance your work reputation.
- If you don't do well in these exams, then you might shut down some possibilities.

Artificial implications are consequences that occur because you choose to impose them, perhaps because of the position you hold:

- Unless your reports come in on time, I will be forced to mark you down on your appraisal.
- If you don't spend more time with your direct reports, then we will have to have a conversation.
- If your timekeeping doesn't improve, then we will have to look at your probation.
- If you don't hit your deadlines, I can't vouch for your promotion.

Be a bit more careful when using these, as they can come across as threats which can sometimes work against collaboration.

6. Narrative is only ever mine

When you deliver adjustment feedback, find ways to deliberately communicate that the feedback comes from a story you've created and is only one perspective amongst others – because that's all it can ever be. This is very powerful and stops people from reacting to assumptions *they think* you've made so you can pre-empt possible undesirable responses. In fact, it allows you to verbalize any assumptions you are making. After all, you've already communicated that you've created the story, you might have made assumptions, and you are just offering information that may or may not help them. Here are several language patterns you might use to achieve this:

- I'm aware this is just my perspective, but...
- I might be wrong but...
- This is the story I'm creating from what I've observed. Feel free to correct it...
- This might be the result of an assumption but...
- Here's my thinking from my perspective...
- It seems to me, from my thinking...
- These are just my thoughts...

I've noticed a marked difference in feedback conversations going well when people utilize this principle and when they don't. It stops the other person from feeling patronized; it removes you from a possible pedestal, as you acknowledge your own limitations, and ultimately builds safety. It's deeply respectful of others and happens to be true. We can only ever see things from our own perspective. There is always a different side of a story. Try it. I promise you won't regret it.

7. Two-way conversation

You always want an adjustment feedback conversation to be two way. Even if you don't have the time right now, you want to ensure that the person hearing it has heard it right and isn't walking away with an un-useful story in their head. Generally, in communication, when you open a loop, it's useful to close it. If it's not two way, how do you know they have heard you? How do you know they have understood your intention?

I remember a former colleague in an organization I worked for making a comment regarding some feedback that was thrown out to the management population by the CEO. The CEO had given some feedback to the group and then walked away. 'It's like throwing a grenade and walking away.' Another participant retorted, 'That's OK. Just put the pin back in!'

When making the conversation two way, make sure you approach the feedback conversation with an attitude of wanting to listen – really listen. It's a dance and if you focus solely on your dance steps – the things you want to share – your combined dance will be out of sync. Have an attitude of true curiosity. And you may have to patiently reiterate your intention, sometimes two, three or even four times before they get the reason and the context of why you are giving the feedback. Try not to defend your story. After all, it is only your story and you, and they will gain more if you identify the differences in both your stories. Sometimes, you will have to negotiate a 'third' story for you to both move on.

One of the things I've noticed in organizations is when people seek the 'truth', in adversarial situations, often it can't be found. One person says one thing. Another says another. They both swear it's the truth. It's a deadlock. That's because we are human and are bound by our perspectives. In feedback situations, it's often better to agree on a version we can all work with and move from there. (of course, there are exceptions, especially if there are legal implications). The goal, after all, is to improve. I've seen too many people waste far too much time trying to establish 'a truth' that is never found. The truth is, of course, necessary for the building of trust, but sometimes the pursuit of it gets in the way.

Use the steps in the PRESENT Model for adjustment feedback. Think of it as wrapping a present that you give to others and finally be present when you deliver it. Noticing how they react will help you to find the best next steps in how you proceed.

In the next chapter, we'll look at a simple tool which will aid you to prepare your seven-step Collaborative Feedback Model at speed.

Recap

- Prepare your adjustment feedback before you give it. It's often more complex than you think. Make sure you're aware of your own internal conflicts. Otherwise, they may hijack the conversation.
- Choose an outcome and make sure it's appropriate for both parties. Make sure it's realistic and use it to set the context.
- Ensure you're in the right type of emotional state to give feedback to avoid the perils of mixed messaging.
- Communicate that the feedback originates from a story you've created. It's not the truth. It's a perception you currently hold.
- Break down your language into what you see and what you hear. Be aware of generalizations. Make it easy for the recipient of feedback to see how you have constructed your story.
- Lay your thinking on the table for all to explore. Link what you've seen and heard to the meaning you've created and then communicate any implications or consequences if they're not already obvious.
- Open it up for a two-way conversation and be ready to listen; to really listen.

CHAPTER 5

PREPARING YOUR FEEDBACK

In the last chapter we talked about how imperative it is to prepare to give adjustment feedback. In fact, it's the first step in the PRESENT Model. It's surprising how seemingly simple feedback can feel complex, especially if you're the type of person who's very sensitive to the needs of others or if you're afraid of conflict. Lots of thoughts and feelings go on inside our minds. Sometimes the feedback we give is relatively simple to think through. Other times it's much harder. What we need is a tried-and-tested tool that helps us to get clarity before and during our feedback conversations.

When we first started exploring Collaborative Feedback in our management training all those years ago, it became clear after many conversations with many managers, what the problems were. They told us about the inbuilt conflict that existed in these adjustment feedback conversations. Not just between the giver and the receiver of feedback, but also the conflict that existed within themselves – a topic we discussed at length in Chapter 2.

What managers requested was a tool to help them prepare and process their feedback, so that they could go into the conversation feeling confident they could be honest and open, as well as being sensitive to the recipient. And the result of that request is what I call the 'Collaborative Feedback Preparation Tool'.

The Preparation Tool is simply a series of five sentence starters. These are very easy to learn, and by completing the sentence starters, most people can process their feedback quite thoroughly.

The tool was designed to implement the successful elements that we've explored in previous chapters. Commit this tool to memory because this tool brings clarity, insight and keeps you on track during your conversations.

Collaborative Feedback Preparation Tool

We'll first introduce you to the tool and then give several examples on how to apply it.

Let me start off by saying that the tool is not a prescribed way to deliver your feedback but to help you *mentally* prepare your feedback. You can use the tool on paper or run it in your mind BEFORE the feedback conversation. The tool is a conversation you have with *yourself* first! Once again, it's also not intended to change people; it's to help you start that conversation in a confident, honest, clear manner.

Here are the sentence starters:

- My outcome is...
- I'm currently feeling... because...
- What I noticed was...
- The meaning I make of that is...
- And that might mean...

That's it – five sentence starters. Say them out loud to yourself several times, and you're halfway there to memorizing them. But how can something so simple solve a problem that feels much more complex? It's because using these sentence starters force you to gain insight and clarity to your own story. We'll explore examples of how to use it in a minute.

Before we do, though, just a word of caution. When I first introduce program participants to the tool, some mistakenly think they must use these phrases to give Collaborative Feedback. Then they make comments like, 'Won't I feel robotic?' and 'It'll be weird if everyone starts giving feedback like this.'

Let me be clear. I am not suggesting that you use the actual language in the tool to deliver your feedback. The sentence starters are for you, the giver of feedback and not for your intended recipient. You're building an internal structure, or scaffolding, on which to articulate an issue. After a while, you'll automatically be processing difficult conversations at speed and can tinker and play with your sentence starters to suit your purposes. If you really don't like the words, you can find alternative sentence starters which serve the same purpose.

Let's explore each of the five sentence starters and see what they do.

1. My outcome is...

When you finish this sentence, focus on what you want the conversation to achieve. Answer it honestly, and it will give you the real context for the feedback. It defines point B, so you can be clear about where you are going, and if, for any reason, you go off track, you can get back. So many people start feedback conversations without really knowing where they want to go with it, which is a recipe for future difficulties.

This sentence starter helps you get clarity on what you are trying to achieve for yourself, the other party and what aspect to focus on. You can start a feedback conversation from many angles, but some are more likely to end in success than others. The critical question to ask here is: What's a good outcome that's likely to end in success?

The other day I saw my daughter eating a bar of chocolate, which caused an immediate sugar craving in my rumbling belly. So I asked her for a small chunk (which is my customary habit). She refused as she had been really looking forward to enjoying the whole bar. I was about to go on a rant on the topic of 'giving' when it dawned on me that I was on the verge of giving feedback. (Sad, I know. In my defence, she is 16 – just in case you think she's a helpless toddler! Still doesn't help my case does it?) I internally started the first sentence of the tool inside my mind: 'My outcome is I want her to be more giving.'

As soon as this thought crossed my mind, I knew how preposterous that was. Is that a realistic starting point for a good conversation? I also thought: *How likely is this bit of feedback going to help her be more giving? And maybe it's good that she's exhibiting assertiveness with her dad!* I chose not to give feedback.

A manager, on one of our programs, shared he was contemplating giving his manager some feedback on his lack of planning. His manager had the habit of dumping tasks on him at the last minute. Following is his thinking using the sentence starter: 'My outcome is I want my manager to think in advance and to consider the consequences of his actions and to realize how insensitive he is. It will also make my life a lot more manageable.'

I had a conversation with the manager on his thinking.

CHRIS: It seems like you have at least two outcomes in mind. You want him first, to consider the consequences of his actions and think ahead rather than at the last minute.

Second, you want him to understand how insensitive he can be.

MANAGER: Yes, I guess so. Actually, it's all one really. I want him to consider the consequences of his actions, realize how insensitive he is and change his behaviours – by thinking in advance and not at the last minute.

CHRIS: Do you think focusing on this particular outcome will make the conversation more productive? Is he likely to receive it well?

MANAGER: No, I can't see him changing. He'll probably be offended.

CHRIS: So, if that's not likely to work, what's another outcome you can hold?

MANAGER: I suppose a better outcome would be to understand why he's doing it and whether there are other pressures on him – like his boss dumping things on him at the last moment.

Afterwards, his starter sentence changed to: 'My outcome is I want to understand why my boss might be giving me last-minute tasks so that it makes my life easier.'

CHRIS: How does your revised outcome sound?

MANAGER: Much better. I feel much more comfortable starting the conversation this way.

And in fact, it turned out to be a very fruitful discussion with his manager.

When you use this first sentence starter, you can begin to assess the likelihood of it bringing about the conversation you really want to talk about. You also gain insight into your own real outcomes, because they aren't always obvious, and you can hold multiple outcomes without knowing it, and some of these may conflict. Sometimes it's more useful to look for intermediate or different outcomes to get to where you want to go. And sometimes you have to take a small step backwards to make a giant leap forward.

2. *I'm currently feeling* [insert feeling] *because* [insert reason]

This is closely connected with the sentence starter above and gives a clue to your current state. This also aids in you getting insight into your true outcome(s). Sometimes we deceive ourselves about the real reason for having the feedback conversation, and as a result, derail ourselves. For example, it may be, the real reason is not that you want them to better themselves, but you are angry at something they did.

The other purpose of this sentence starter is that it acts as a warning system for whether you should proceed in your current state of mind or not. Think of it as a set of traffic lights: red, amber, green!

The number-one thing that derails your feedback conversation is, giving it while you are feeling frustrated, angry or some other similar emotion. The other person will pick up your state, and their defences will subconsciously kick into action. So, if your sentence starter goes something like this:

I'm currently feeling… [for example, very irritated] because… [for example, they've broken their promise to me].

There are several things you can do.

You can delay giving the feedback if it's at all possible or in your preparation reframe the situation by telling yourself something like,

- From time to time, I've made mistakes too.
- I won't remember this in 10 years.
- In the grand scheme of things, it's a minor blip.

Finally, there's also one psychological insight that makes a tremendous difference if you fully realize the implication behind it. When you get irritated or frustrated, it's because one of your expectations, values or standards has been infringed upon. Think about it. Is that not true? If that standard never existed, you wouldn't be irritated right now. But who created that standard? Whether consciously or not? You! This might be a hard thing to accept – ultimately, you created your own irritation and, in realizing that, let it go. People who truly get this, take ownership and responsibility to a whole different level.

But please don't get me wrong. I'm not saying we should relinquish expectations, values or standards because they are vital for an organization to function effectively and efficiently. You need to drive to uphold and improve them. What I am saying is that understanding the psychology behind these things can help you to manage your own emotional state as you enter feedback conversations.

Get into the right kind of state before you give feedback. One great state to adopt is curiosity. Curiosity is potent. It invites people in and opens up possibilities. And if you're wondering how to get into that state, here's one easy technique.

Think about something that makes you curious. It can be anything that makes you wonder. One of the questions I sometimes ask is, 'How the hell can we largely be made up of space?' (Atoms are comprised mainly of space. Atoms make up molecules, molecules organs etc.) or 'Why do cars suddenly slow down on fast roads for no apparent reason?' (If you know the answer to these questions, please don't tell me; I like the feeling these questions give me. It keeps the sense of curiosity even in my ignorance.) Thinking about these types of things can give you the feeling of wonderment and inquisitiveness, which you can then transfer into the task at hand. We'll explore this in more depth in the next chapter.

Entering adjustment feedback conversations in the wrong state will increase the risk of it not going as well as you might wish.

3. What I noticed was...

This next sentence starter will force you to break down your packaged judgements, assumptions and labels into things that you actually saw and heard. This then enables you to get insight into how you constructed your story. Then you can decide if your story even warrants an adjustment feedback conversation.

There have been many times when I've become clear about the validity of my own story and stopped myself from giving feedback. Forcing yourself to break down your packaged assumptions into things you can see or hear will give you the clarity to articulate elements that can be acted upon. Sometimes your packaged judgements and labels will have several layers so the trick is to keep going until you can imagine seeing it or hearing it in your mind.

One manager I worked with, had a colleague who had the habit of seemingly prolonging meetings unnecessarily. He was thinking of giving her feedback and asked me for some coaching. I asked him to run through the Preparation Tool, and we got to this sentence starter.

> MANAGER: I've noticed she's very inefficient in her communication and seems to wind people up.
>
> CHRIS: What do you mean when you use the words 'inefficient', 'communication' and 'wind people up'?
>
> MANAGER: She switches topic before finishing the first. She pauses for a long time mid-sentence. I've noticed, on at least four occasions, where she's waited until the last two minutes before the scheduled end of the meeting to bring up critical questions.

As the manager began processing the information, he had some insights about what he could address and what he couldn't. In the end, he settled for an alternative course of action – being clearer about meeting etiquette and agreeing on some rules of engagement.

Another program participant, Joan, felt stressed because she had been advised to have a conversation with her manager because she felt like her manager was giving her very little space.

> JOAN: I've noticed that my manager patronises me. She micromanages me, and it makes me feel very claustrophobic.
>
> CHRIS: What do you mean when you use the words 'patronizes' and 'micromanages'?
>
> JOAN: By patronizes I mean, she tells me things in a 'headmistress' tone that I already know. For goodness sake, I've been in the industry for 25 years… And by micromanages,

I mean she questions me at least three times a week regarding how I am implementing processes.

CHRIS: 'Headmistress tone'?

JOAN: Yes, it's like an order that I might give my 10-year-old child.

Notice when you start to break things down into what you can see or hear, it may give insight on what you can initially address and what you cannot.

Breaking things down ensures you get to the right amount of specificity that will enable the recipient of the feedback to do something about it – if they are inclined to do so. It's hard to change being '*patronising*'. It's much easier to change your tone.

Break information down into
what you can see and hear.

4: The meaning I make of that is...

This sentence starter, to some extent, works back the opposite way to the previous sentence starter - 'What I noticed was...' As you use the entire tool, you'll notice that you'll begin to work on this sentence starter when you're answering the previous sentence starter because they go hand in hand. How else can you pick out what you've noticed?

So why is this particular sentence starter necessary? Because it provides a wider context for your story. It allows you to expose your thinking and lay down your thoughts for all to examine. The wider context can seep into the feedback conversation, and if you're not aware of it, it can once again alter the dynamics of your interaction.

It gives you distance and a broader perspective from your own psychological inner workings, which then enables you to process your thinking more objectively and effectively. It's the heart of how you construct your mental narrative and gives you clarity on how to lay out your story on the floor for all to explore. Doing this is tremendously powerful and sends an empowering message to those who receive it. It also clarifies the story you have created for yourself. If it's unclear, you can't communicate it. If it's flawed, it enables you to abandon embarking on the conversation in the first place. So, carrying on from the example above:

> JOAN: What I notice is that she tells me things in an imperative tone that I already know and asks me questions at least three times a week about how I am implementing the process. The meaning I make of that is... my manager is a micromanager, we don't get on, and she'll never change

5: And that might mean...

Once again, you might notice how these sentence starters blend into one another. This sentence starter invites you to cast your mind into the future and draw out implications from the meaning you've made of the data you've noticed. It's another layer of broadening out your own story. It's a form of self-coaching and can often shed light as to the conflicts you might be experiencing.

Continuing Joan's story:

> JOAN: What I notice is that she tells me things in an imperative tone that I already know and asks me questions at least three times a week about how I am implementing the process. The meaning I make of that is my manager is

a micromanager, we don't get on, and she'll never change. **And that might mean** we'll have conflict when having the conversation. She will get upset, so I can't have the conversation. I will feel bad, and she'll never change. That will frustrate me until I can't take any more and I can't take it further to her manager because I will feel disloyal and eventually, I will have to leave. [*Joan then went very quiet.*] I'm making quite a few assumptions here, aren't I?

CHRIS: Like?

JOAN: She's a micromanager... whereas she could just be employing a directive style of management. After all, I'm relatively new to the company, although I've been in the industry for a long time. Also, I'm assuming she will never change. Perhaps she's doing this on purpose – until I'm familiar with the processes? And I'm worrying about nothing.

What great insights. Notice as you finish the sentence starter you are laying your own story on the floor for yourself to examine. With a bit of practice, you'll begin to find the assumptions you make – because as human beings, it's in our nature to make them. And you'll also discover insights about your own thinking. This will also help you diffuse unwanted emotion and increase the likelihood of you coming across as a rational, strategic and insightful person when you come to deliver the feedback. There's something about getting your story clarified. It's stark. You can verbalize it and explore it with yourself or someone you trust in confidence.

In the end, Joan decided to change the nature of the conversation and had a conversation that went something like this:

JOAN: I notice that you're very detailed in your management of me at the moment. I also notice that you're very directive and clear in your instructions – perhaps because I'm new. I haven't had other managers be so detailed. Will this always be the case?

MANAGER: Good gracious no. I just have to make sure that you're clear on the processes and following them correctly. You're doing great. I'd love to be able to always spend this amount of time with you, but we're really stretched right now. I do this with all newcomers.

Joan was relieved, and their relationship grew in leaps and bounds.

Commonly asked questions

Now we've gone through the Preparation Tool, there's a couple of questions that people on my program frequently ask that I would like to answer:

Q: Do you have to do the sentence starters in strict sequence?

A: You can start with any of the first three sentence starters because it won't make any difference. Sentence starters 3, 4 and 5, however, lend themselves to being asked in sequence.

Q: Does the wording of the sentence starters have to be exact?

A: We've played around with the sentence starters – trying different combinations. The answer, strictly speaking, is no, but the idea is to build an internal structure that elicits the same types of information from your inner world. To process your feedback in real time, the sentence starters need almost to be automatic or second nature. But feel free to insert your own words into the sentence starters.

In my experience, the five sentence starters have been well tested and are reasonably robust to apply to most situations. And the feedback I've received about the Preparation Tool is that it gives clarity in several areas:

- The inner conflict you are experiencing.
- The story you are creating so that you can lay it out for others to see.
- The bigger story surrounding your initial story.
- Insights into self and your own thinking and development.
- Which outcome to concentrate on, to have the best chance of success,
- Understanding whether you even need to give feedback or not.

You've probably realized this isn't *just* a Feedback Tool but can be used to generate clarity in a huge range of scenarios but more about that in Chapter 9.

Using the tool to give adjustment feedback

Finally, in this chapter, let's look at a couple more examples of how the tool might be used and both are incidences of me preparing feedback to give to people. One is an example from business and the other an example from home.

A few years ago, I had a strong compulsion to give some feedback to a client. He was a CEO who had engaged me as a consultant in a change-management project that wasn't going well. I noticed the CEO was continually complaining about the competence of his executive team members, and they were not getting things done, which had been agreed at the team meetings. The same team members, however, were telling me a different story. They were saying the CEO was changing decisions after the decisions had been made and as a result, were paralysed by confusion. They couldn't understand why he was undermining the decision-making process but felt powerless to stop him. I felt like I needed to bring this up with the CEO, but also sensed, I needed to be very careful, so I duly employed the Collaborative Feedback Preparation Tool:

My outcome is to challenge the CEO to stop changing decisions out of the boardroom and to help him have clarity about the competence of his team so that we can all make things run more smoothly.

I'm currently feeling very calm and determined, but cautious **because** some of these issues are sensitive to people.

I notice others are telling a different story to the CEO, and I notice that the CEO is often complaining about his executive team and their capabilities. (e.g. They're not strategic. They don't think things through). I notice the volume and tone of his voice change as he complains. I notice that other team members say that the CEO changes decisions without letting them know. I hear them say that they don't have conversations about this. I notice at the team meetings I attend that these topics are not brought to the agenda.

The meaning I make of this is due to these issues, the change initiative will be hindered. It will put a strain on the relationships of the team and tear down trust. Because of that, communication will get more challenging which will result in a whole host of other problems, all of which work against the change initiative.

And that might mean everyone loses: things that need to get done, don't get done and might even result in more turnover of staff, resulting in catastrophic loss of organizational knowledge.

As my story became clearer and clearer, it helped me to focus on the thing that might produce the most leverage. After all, giving feedback on all these things might muddy the picture. Also, I gained insight about focusing on some outcomes that might be initially too challenging (I realize, of course, that I might be making assumptions about people's abilities to deal with situations!). In the end, it became clear to me what I should initially focus on. Below is the feedback conversation I had with the CEO, and I've inserted commentary to shine a light on the feedback approach. I approached the CEO, and our conversation went like this:

> CHRIS: Is now a good time to have a chat about some things I've noticed that might help the change initiative go better? [*Making the outcome explicit.*]
>
> CEO: Yes, sure.
>
> CHRIS: I've noticed from my conversations with some of the other exec team members, they think that – from time to time – decisions change without them being informed [*notice the see/hear language*]. And this seems to result in confusion of agreements made within the exec meetings, which results in tasks not being done and things falling behind in the change strategy. I've also noticed in the

meetings I've attended that the conversations needed to address this issue are not being had... And that might mean the problems might continue, or even magnify. Of course, this just might be my perspective, and I'm missing things in the story I've created. [*Letting him know this is just a story, I've created to help with safety – the narrative is only ever mine.*] What do you think?

CEO: That's interesting. Let's talk.

And we had a great conversation about some of the ongoing issues. The preparation allowed me to confidently and succinctly lay some of the issues on the table for us to explore. Some of these issues can get complex and having a tool to sort the complexity is invaluable.

Here's another example. A short while ago, I was driving back home, and I pulled into the road where I live. As I did so, I saw three teenage boys playing a manic ball game right next to where the cars were parked and right by where I was going to park my car. Immediately I could feel my heart sink and started having visions of smashed car windows and dented bonnets. I confess I had a bit of anxiousness about addressing these kinds of situations, formed from my own teenage years of recklessness.

You see, years back, in my teenage days, my friend and I were playing a ball game in the neighbourhood when a man came charging outside of his house and told us all to go away (actually in much more colourful language), or he would call the police. We were much aggrieved and took great delight painting his windows black and calling different taxicabs to his house day and night while sitting on the swings in the park opposite, looking on in delight.

So, you understand my dilemma, even though some of you might be thinking, 'Justice' in your heart. I know – I deserve that. And I'm truly sorry now.

So, how to address this situation without upping the risk of retribution? I quickly began processing the feedback:

My outcome is I would like them to stop playing in that spot.

I'm currently feeling a bit anxious about having the conversation **because** they might not take it well.

I notice they are playing a ball game and it is close to the cars and I notice from time to time the ball going astray and bouncing near the cars

The meaning I make of this is that it's highly likely they will cause some damage.

And that might mean dealing with the consequences of going to their houses to confront them and their parents about compensation for damages and causing tension in the neighbourhood and possibly dealing with retribution afterwards from the teenage kids.

As I looked at my own story that I had been creating, I realized I needed to be careful to frame the right outcome. The Preparation Tool also helped form the words in which to handle it.

After parking my car, I went up to them and said:

> ME: Hey, lads, sorry to bother you because it looks like you're having a lot of fun. I've noticed in the last couple of minutes that the ball is bouncing close to those cars. I'm a bit worried that it might accidentally hit one of them. I'm just trying to keep property safe and not spoil your fun. Of course, I might be a bit paranoid, and the ball might never hit them. Does that sound reasonable? What do you think?

KIDS: [*Nodding.*]

ME: In that case, would you mind moving your game around the corner?

They nodded their heads and 20 seconds later, they moved down the road. And to date, no one has painted my windows black, nor have I had unsolicited taxis pull outside my door.

The Preparation Tool enabled me to be much more articulate and confident about what I was going to say. It also helped me to choose an outcome that was more likely to produce a result – not to stop their game, but to move to a safer place. Notice that by using the Preparation Tool, the words come to mind much more easily because there is clarity in the story.

But some of you might be thinking, 'This is a bit long winded. Can't you just say something simple like, 'Kids can you move please, because you might damage the cars?'

Well, you could. And on another day, I might have. And the result might be the same. But we're talking about Collaborative Feedback. And sometimes the issues are more complex. You are trying to maximize the chances of engagement. By laying your thinking out in a transparent way, you build trust – by building trust, you increase the chances of the input being accepted and getting the outcome you're shooting for. It also minimizes the chance of being misunderstood.

How to best utilize the tool

As I've said previously, the best way to use the tool is to think of it like a scaffolding that informs your feedback conversation. You won't always need to use it, but it will be there when there are more complex issues when you need clarity or if giving feedback feels a bit risky.

When I train the tool in my feedback programs, I get participants to initially apply the tool as much as possible – even five or ten times a day to situations. (You'd be surprised at how much you do give feedback without knowing it.) After a while, it becomes automatic, and you'll find your preparation happening with ease. Then you'll discover how much easier it is to find the appropriate approach and language to focus on during your feedback.

I hope you find the Collaborative Feedback Preparation Tool super useful – easy to implement and an insightful guide to those difficult feedback conversations.

Recap

- The Preparation Tool isn't prescriptive but can help you *mentally* prepare your feedback – either on paper or run it in your mind BEFORE the feedback conversation.
- The tool is not intended to help you to change other people but to start that change conversation in a confident, honest, clear manner.
- Give adjustment feedback by the five starter sentences and 3, 4 and 5 lend themselves to being asked in sequence.

CHAPTER 6

DELIVERING ADJUSTMENT FEEDBACK SUCCESSFULLY

So far, we've explored the elements of good feedback, we've covered the PRESENT Model for Collaborative Feedback and looked at a tool for helping you prepare feedback. It's one thing to prepare your feedback well and another thing to deliver it with success. This chapter will cover things to look out for and tips for the actual delivery of feedback. It's a compilation of things that commonly crop up for participants in my programs that I've collected over the years.

This chapter will cover topics such as getting into the right state, how to start a feedback conversation, some tips for building extra safety, some alternatives to language patterns and several frequently asked questions.

Getting into the right state

When we embark on giving adjustment feedback, we are inviting the recipient into a conversation. We're giving them an offer. We're saying, 'Hey I've got some things you might want to look at, that might help you. Do you want to see?' As I described in a previous chapter, it's got to be done invitingly or it stands a good chance of being declined. To be compelling, you must get into the right physical and emotional state. If you don't, then there's a high chance you'll hijack your choice of words and train of thought. As you might imagine, angry, frustrated and unconfident states don't lend themselves well to compelling invitations.

Our states change continuously. Even as I write, I notice I go from bored to frustrated, to elated, to thoughtful, to determined. And my body physically reflects what I'm emotionally feeling, albeit subtly.

So how do we get into the right kinds of physical and emotional states? Well, first, physical and emotional states are highly connected – change one, and you will affect the other. There are lots of ways to change your state, but before we do that, let's quickly explore some appropriate states for giving adjustment feedback.

So back to our invitation metaphor. What makes you want to accept an invitation from someone? Perhaps when that person is warm and friendly, non-judgmental, and even excited to have you there. One powerful state I've already described is curiosity. I have a vivid memory of my brother inviting me to taste some Space-Dust (popping candy) when I was little. 'I wonder what this tastes like?' he said to me. 'I bet it's really cool.' I could sense his curiosity, inviting me compellingly and soon I was infected. Curiosity is powerful and contagious! You'll find it's also impossible to be curious and angry, frustrated or judgmental at the same time. Try it and see.

What's useful in purposely altering your states is taking yourself through a routine. Sportspeople do this regularly. They need to get into an appropriate state to perform at their best.

Altering your state

You can develop your own routines, but here's one that seems to work:

1. Take a few deep diaphragmatic breaths. Breathe through your nose into your belly and out through your nose or mouth. (When you breathe in, your belly should

push out. If you want, put your hand flat on your belly, and you should feel it being pushed out and not upward.)

2. Feel the gravity push you down into the ground, if you are standing. If you are sitting, feel gravity push down through your backside.
3. Think of a time when you were curious, warm or friendly. Step into the memory as if you were there and see what you saw, hear what you heard and feel what you felt. For most people, you should begin to start noticing a change in your emotional state.
4. Transfer that feeling to the matter at hand. Just be curious about the story you created when preparing feedback. Wonder at how you created it and be curious about how another perspective might feel and look.
5. Finally, imagine the feedback interaction going well and the person you've given it to, enthusiastically exploring your story

If this routine doesn't work for you, try inventing one of your own. Go for a walk. Look at nature and connect. Try changing the speed of your breathing by slowing it down. But do what it takes to get into a useful state for giving feedback.

How to start the feedback conversation

Many people get nervous right at the start of the feedback conversation if they perceive the feedback is going to be tricky. I often ask participants on my program, 'How do you normally start the conversation?'

A few common responses are:

- Do you mind if I give you some feedback?
- Is now a good time to give you feedback?
- Can we have a chat about something, please?

I ask people who volunteer these answers, 'What response do you get?' And it depends, of course; upon the people involved, their relationship, the environment in which they are in and the feedback culture in the organization. However, a typical response is when they use any of the above phrases as a starter to the feedback conversation, they notice an awkward silence, a small gulp, a deep breath or a slight look of panic. All these might be indicators of people going into protection mode. And for Collaborative Feedback, we want to ensure as much as possible that we use communication that helps people stay out of protection mode. It may not always be possible to stop them going into that mode, because of the nature of the conversation, their personal tendencies or the current environment. However, we can do things to reduce the likelihood.

People can get defensive at the start of feedback, so for collaborative conversations, it's imperative to take them out of it as soon as possible.

But why do these phrases invite people into protection mode? Well, partly because they are too generic. It sends people's minds off into a search for everything they've done wrong, with no hint of context and they are immediately creating several stories inside of their heads. The feeling of uncertainty is invoked, and the body begins to react.

Another common way to start a feedback conversation is to ask questions. Here's one example a manager described to me about trying to give some feedback to a staff member to improve their report writing.

MANAGER: How was the report you handed in last week?

STAFF MEMBER: Good.

MANAGER: Do you think it was well constructed?

STAFF MEMBER: I think so.

MANAGER: Do you think it could have been presented better?

STAFF MEMBER: Why, do you?

Asking questions to start off a feedback conversation can have the drawback of feeling like you are in an interrogation. You, as the giver of feedback, can sound like you are treading on eggshells or lacking confidence or worse, trying to manipulate the agenda. As you ask the questions, people ask inside their own heads, 'Where is this going?'

One final example of a common way to start the conversation is the 'sandwich technique,' which we talked about earlier. If you remember, it goes something like this:

1. Say something positive about the person.
2. Give feedback on the stuff you want them to change.
3. End by saying something positive about the person.

This technique can work occasionally, but it has its drawbacks. Many people voice discomfort at doing it this way. The technique intends to help people feel good about themselves while addressing things that need changing. That's not necessarily a bad thing. It also has an underlying message that says, 'Hey, while looking at the things you need to change, don't forget the good things about yourself.' People often take the things they need to change out of proportion, and the sandwich technique firmly puts it back into balance. Here's one real-life example, I heard from a participant:

> MANAGER: Hey, can I give you some feedback? Firstly, you are doing great, and I appreciate your hard work in the marketing campaign.
>
> PARTICIPANT: Thanks.
>
> MANAGER: You do, however, need to be a bit more careful in the way you speak to your colleagues.
>
> PARTICIPANT: Oh...
>
> MANAGER: But, generally, you're doing great, and I'm sure it's making a difference in the department.

So, what do you think? Well, it does avoid magnifying the issue but here are some possible drawbacks:

- It can send a mixed message and leave the recipient confused and asking, 'What exactly are we talking about?'
- The recipient can feel manipulated and think, 'Why don't you say what you really want to say, instead of playing games?' (In the UK, the technique is also commonly, unofficially referred to as 'The 'shirt' sandwich!' (without the 'r'! Pardon my language!)

It's important to frame the feedback conversation in a way that communicates openness, honesty and transparency

– as well as building safety. The recipient must also be in no doubt as to the intention of the conversation and know where the conversation is going.

So, what are some alternatives to the starters above? First, remember feedback is a gift. You are making an offer – therefore frame it as such. Next, I recommend utilizing one of the principles discussed in an earlier chapter right at the very start – build safety by communicating the outcome and subsequent context. So here it is:

> *Start with a sentence that communicates the intended outcome – this then is your context.*

And remember it's more useful if you pick an outcome that is agreeable to you both – but it doesn't mean that it can't be a challenging one. Below are a few examples. See what you think?

- Can we discuss how we can make your presentation even better? (The outcome is to make the presentation better. Most people would sign up to that.)
- Can we have a discussion so that I can properly understand our performance on the project? (Understanding performance is the outcome here, not improving performance. Notice the subtle difference.)
- Can we have a chat about our perceptions regarding your performance on the project? (The outcome here is making the different perceptions explicit.)
- Can we have a chat about how to improve your performance next month? (Notice here the outcome

is a bit more challenging and there are inbuilt assumptions – i.e. the performance needs to improve and in the following month.)

- Just so we can have shared expectations, can we chat about what just happened? (The outcome is understanding. It's not only about them. It's about us.)
- Just so that we can have clarity about our agreement... (The outcome here is clarity.)

If you pick up signals that the recipient is still going into protective mode, you can follow it up by clarifying your intention or clarifying what your intention is not. Remember it's a dance – if they back up, you move with them; if they move forward, you respond appropriately – so there's no resistance.

> YOU: Can we have a chat on how to improve your performance in the next month?
>
> THEM: [*Eyes open wider. Gulp.*]
>
> YOU: Oh, it's not that you're doing badly. It's just that you said you wanted to aim to be doing your best always, so we are just exploring ways to improve.

Or

> YOU: Can we have a conversation about how to improve performance in the next month?
>
> THEM: [*Eyes open wider. Gulp.*]
>
> YOU: Oh, it's just about having a clear understanding of performance standards and seeing where we need to go from there.

Sometimes you may have to go through three, four or even more iterations of clarification. You'll find the other person may keep going into protection mode, but if you stay patient and keep clarifying the outcome, they'll finally get on the same page. If you advance without a common understanding of why you are giving the feedback, it may end un-collaboratively.

One final hint about outcomes. If you're struggling to find a suitable outcome for your feedback conversation, a couple that almost always work is 'understanding' and 'clarity'. Of course, they are different expressions of the same intention. Here are a couple of examples:

- Can we have a conversation so I can get a bit of clarity about [*insert topic*]?
- Can we have a chat so we can be on the same page regarding [*insert topic]*?

Notice the subtlety in the outcome here. It's no longer about them – it's about clarity for you in the first instance. In the second example, it's also not just about them – it's about us being on the same page.

Finally, you might want to couple the outcome-focused starter with a phrase that communicates it's only one perspective among others – it's just your outlook. Remember, the 'narrative is only ever mine'.

'Can we have a chat to take your performance even higher?' becomes 'Can we have a chat to take your performance even higher? I have some thoughts that might be useful, and of course, it's just my perspective.'

This adjustment has the added element of safety and invites an offer of exploration. Giving feedback is always an offer – and the more enticing you can make it, the more likely it is to be taken.

If you want an easy way to remember the elements in your opening gambit (I know some of you out there love mnemonic devices), try remembering the three O's:

- Offer - asking for engagement
- Outcome - making explicit point B
- Outlook - this is just one perspective amongst others

You might be asking, 'Do you have to frame the conversation at the start? Can't you just go into the feedback?'

The answer is, yes you can, depending on the type of relationship you have with the person you are giving the feedback to, the regular dynamics that occur between you and a whole host of other factors. Going into the feedback directly without setting context can, however, raise the risk of it going wrong. People begin to ask themselves, 'Why are we talking about this?' If you don't give them a reason and a context, it increases the chances of the conversation being derailed.

Pay attention to how you start the conversation. I find it's particularly important when I am giving feedback to my teenage children. If I don't take the time to think through how I start, I usually hear footsteps running off into the distance or a breakout into World War III.

A word on language

One of the things I'm nearly always asked about when I train the PRESENT Model of Collaborative Feedback and its preparation tool is, 'Won't I sound like a robot if I use this method?'

The answer in a word is 'No.' The Preparation Tool is simply a template for you to prepare your feedback. It's a scaffolding on which to erect your building/feedback. Once prepared, you can swap the words in the structure for similar words that convey the same meaning.

You can if you wish, use the language in the Preparation Tool; it won't sound unnatural to others. People won't know you're using the model. (In fact, you don't even have to use the model at all. Just being aware of the model and preparing your feedback using the tool will give you guidance on how to go about it.)

One of the things I do on the program is to teach the PRESENT Model and the Preparation Tool and then use it on the delegates to give feedback to them as they are learning it. I always ask, 'I've been using the PRESENT Model on you the whole day. Did you notice that I did?' Very few people do.

But I know we are all different, some of us want variety, so in the back of the book in Appendix 1, I've listed some alternatives you can use to install the scaffolding. There are phrases to open, to build safety, to convey intention, to communicate you are just telling your story.

Use the appendix to come up with your combinations to make the conversation as natural as possible for you.

The art of building safety

We've talked a lot about building safety into the feedback conversation in previous chapters because it's a fundamental cornerstone of Collaborative Feedback. As I've already described, being nervous, fearful, careful or in protection mode doesn't lend itself to a collaborative conversation.

Of course, some people are by nature, friendlier and more approachable. They tend to smile more, be a bit chattier and project a warm persona. If you're one of these people, then you'll probably find you don't have to make as much effort to build safety. If you're not, then you'll just have to work that little bit harder.

Sometimes, you may find you have to spend more time in building safety before moving on to the issue at hand. And often you'll find you may need to go back and keep building the safety net. An example of this was shared by a manager who was giving feedback to one of her direct reports, a customer service advisor. The direct report had a reputation of being a little bit 'prickly' and previous mis-communication had exacerbated the situation. Something had gone wrong with the customer complaint process, but it wasn't clear where the problem lay. The direct report had responsibility for ensuring the process went smoothly, but the manager had a hunch that she hadn't taken ownership of the situation. After going through the Collaborative Feedback Model, the manager had the insight that she would suspend her assumptions and first thoroughly find out what was going on.

MANAGER: Can we have a chat to find out what's going on with this complaint to see if we can figure it out?

DIRECT REPORT: Operations keep messing this up. I'm doing my best. It's not my fault.

MANAGER: I'm sure you are doing your best. Please don't get me wrong. I'm not looking to attribute blame. I'm just trying to understand the situation first before we do anything.

DIRECT REPORT: Yeah but it's not fair that they point the finger at me.

MANAGER: I assure you; I'm not pointing the finger. We just need to figure out what's going on.

DIRECT REPORT: Oh, OK.

MANAGER: I notice… [followed by the feedback using the PRESENT Model].

The conversation went smoothly for a little while before the direct report began to once again, deny responsibility as they were exploring facts.

MANAGER: Hey, I might be misinterpreting, but I notice that we seem to be using language that seems to be allocating blame again. Once again, I'm not having a go, or issuing blame. We just need to understand what's going on.

In this incidence, the manager backtracked so they could advance with safety. She had to do this several times. The manager had kept her eyes and ears open as they were talking. She hadn't focused solely on what she wanted to get across but realized they were in a dance. She took the liberty of interpreting any signs of defensiveness, aggression or silence as signs of lack of safety and then took appropriate steps to build more safety.

Interpret any signs of defensiveness, aggression or silence as lack of safety.

And after a little while, the conversation took an interesting turn. As they were exploring the situation, the direct report began to see how her lack of actions had contributed to the problem. The rest of the conversation went well, and the problem was eventually solved.

In our model in Chapter 4, we primarily address the safety issue by making explicit the outcome, communicating it's just our story and that we are aware we might be making assumptions.

Aarav built a fantastic safety net, and the feedback conversation developed a delightful flavour of its own.

Power dynamics

We can't talk about safety without talking about power. Power plays a massive part in all communications, whether we like it or not. Power is a very real thing and undoubtedly distorts communications and behaviours. We can't deny it has an effect. We are all influenced by it. Our emotional and physical states change when power comes into play. Power can play a big part in making us feel unsafe as the receiver of feedback. Power can also make us inappropriately overconfident as the giver of feedback if we hold a position of power. Recognizing this can help feedback conversations go better.

The scary thing about power is we're often blind to it. As the holder of power, we don't realize its effect. As the non-power holder, we just feel its effects subconsciously. As leaders in an organization, our goals are to deliver the value propositions (the benefits that our products or services provide) as effectively and efficiently as possible to maximize value. This can only occur through people who work for and with the organization. You want this system of operations to run with as little friction as possible. For this to happen, you must give regular, continuous feedback, both up, down and sideways through the chain of command. The more friction there is, the more fractured the relationships, and the less effective and efficient the delivery of the value proposition. As a manager, it's vital that everyone who works below you in the hierarchy can deliver feedback back up to you. It's in your interests to enable this to happen.

I've known several CEOs who have told their staff, 'My door is always open. Please come and talk to me.' And there's very little take up. Why? Well, depending on the culture, the power factor can be a huge hindrance.

When you give feedback to someone lower in the power chain, you have to really consider building safety – that is, if you want a genuinely collaborative response. Many people have shared the types of thoughts that run wild inside their minds when getting feedback from a person with more power in the hierarchy. Some of these are listed below:

- Am I going to be ostracized?
- Am I going to get sacked?

- There goes my chance of promotion!
- Oh no. He doesn't like me.
- I knew I was rubbish.
- Who's told on me?
- I've got to be careful with what I say here.
- Kill me now.

I don't want to scare you but, I'm not kidding about the last comment either! Be prepared as the power holder to keep going back to building safety. You may have to do this several times in the same conversation to get to a truly collaborative place.]

Paolo was confused by David's reaction because he didn't realize his tone and body language secretly distorted/controlled the conversation.

Giving adjustment feedback to someone with more power

What's interesting to me is that it works the other way around too. If you are much lower in the organizational hierarchy with less power, you also must build safety. Why? Because those who hold more power are often unaware of the power stories that are playing in their minds. There are stories of, 'I must be respected; you can't talk to me this way; you have no right to challenge me, etc.'

Pay attention to the tone of voice of people in different levels of organizations as they talk to each other. Those in higher positions often communicate with lower tones and imperative language patterns to those with less power.

You see it in families too. I notice my own tone with my grown-up son and almost grown-up daughter. As hard as I try, I often automatically fall into using imperative tones and language, which cause unnecessary conflict in the household.

What these imperative tones and language patterns do, is they communicate, 'think twice before challenging me. It's clearly not your place.' This makes giving adjustment feedback so much more challenging and difficult.

A common mistake I see in response to this dynamic is, when staff lower in the hierarchy get an opportunity to have a feedback conversation with those higher up, they end up pouring out a string of grievances – which comes across as a string of complaints and not a useful feedback conversation.

There are two reasons why it's beneficial for you to prepare feedback for someone who has more power than you:

1. You are more likely to be in a stressed state, which may make you less eloquent with your words and the way

you come across with your tones and body language. Therefore, you must spend some focus on getting your state right.

2. You need to be clear about what you are trying to achieve and keep the conversation on track. That is if you don't want to come across as unclear or confused or worse still – bitter.

Taking time to really understand and relay back

One of the best ways to build safety is to make sure that the other person feels heard. You can do this by summarizing or paraphrasing what you think they are communicating to you and not moving on before they acknowledge that you do indeed, understand the heart of what they're saying. One way to do this is by using the phrase, 'Are you saying/thinking/communicating...?'

Let me share an example of how an associate built some feedback safety for me. It was regarding the late submission of a proposal.

ASSOCIATE: I noticed that the proposal missed the deadline.

CHRIS: Yes, but it was given to me very late.

ASSOCIATE: Are you thinking that I'm insinuating blame because that's not my intention

CHRIS: No, not really.

ASSOCIATE: Oh, sorry. I misunderstood. What was your thinking?

CHRIS: I was really annoyed at myself for missing the deadline.

ASSOCIATE: Oh, so you were expressing how annoyed you were at yourself?

CHRIS: Yes.

ASSOCIATE: I was just bringing it up to see what we could learn as a team to improve the way we go about proposals.

CHRIS: Oh, OK.

Notice he didn't move on until I had acknowledged he had fully understood what I was communicating. I see so many problems caused in areas of customer service when customer service agents say things like, 'I understand what you are saying...' and then move on to voice their perspective before the customer feels that the agent has understood. It's much more effective not to move on until they've acknowledged you've truly heard them. You can do this by summarizing or parroting what you think they've said. You'll know you've got there when they say things like, 'That's right' or 'Yes, you've got it'. You'll also hear a change of tone and/or see a difference in body language.

Do not move on until the other person acknowledges they feel understood. When people feel like you've heard and understood them, it builds excellent safety. It's a critical part of the dance.

Tips for Collaborative Feedback

We've covered several important principles regarding the delivery of the feedback you've prepared. Following are a few tips to deal with a variety of everyday situations.

Tip 1: Dealing with particularly 'prickly' people

From time to time, people ask how to deal with people who are particularly sensitive to adjustment feedback. You know what I'm talking about here – the type of person who seems to react to the smallest suggestion of criticism. They seem to misread the tiniest of comments and blow up at the smallest of things. You feel you must be particularly sensitive; you have to choose your words carefully, or it could all go wrong. Often, it's much easier to not have these conversations at all with this 'type' of person.

First, it's important to understand, if you believe someone is 'prickly', it raises the tension for you the feedback giver. You put yourself on edge and therefore must be particularly careful with managing your own state so that your tension doesn't come out in your vocal tone or body language. Sometimes it helps to realize, even if you consider someone as 'prickly', they might describe it as something else.

For example, I had the fortune of having a conversation with someone who had been labelled as 'prickly' by others in the organization – let's call him Fred. A colleague had given him feedback that he was tough to give feedback to, as he seemed to react out of proportion. The colleague had used the word 'prickly'. This left Fred confused and a little bit angry. We explored some behaviours in a coaching conversation, and Fred's opinion about himself emerged. It went something like this: 'I don't consider myself particularly hard to talk to. I know some people seem to think that and they say I react. But I'm my own harshest critic. I listen to what people say, but I can't seem to help myself. I just have very high standards.' It transpires Fred wasn't reacting against the person who had given him feedback. He was reacting against himself. Who can accurately guess the inner stories that people create? Therefore, it's even more important that we make clear it's our story that we've created and simply lay the information down for them to see.

So how do we specifically go about dealing with people who seem to exhibit these types of behaviours? Don't make a special case for them. Don't label them and take care to use the safety principles. Here they are once again:

1. Do your preparation so you are clear what you are trying to achieve and choose an outcome that will give you more chance of success.
2. Keep restating what the conversation is about and what it is not.
3. Use language which communicates that it is your story and your perspective. Make it clear you are aware that there may be assumptions in your stories.
4. Keep going back and building safety if necessary, by repeating steps 2–3. You may have to do this several times.
5. Get curious about their story and make sure they feel heard and understood, and don't move on until they say they acknowledge that explicitly.
6. Try your best not to react to their tone and body language.

Tip 2: Don't try and solve a problem before you've explored and understood it

When we give Collaborative Feedback to others, we are inviting them to jointly explore the problem. If you try and give solutions before the problem is agreed upon, the recipient of feedback can interpret it as you making assumptions. It sends the message, I've already come to my conclusions. I know what's wrong - here's how to solve it. Even if you are right, this approach does not tend to invite a two-way conversation.

Another manager, Tim, was a director of a software company. He described an 'unsuccessful' feedback conversation with one of his staff, Mike. Mike had a conflict with John in a different department. John was critical to Tim's department hitting a critical deadline.

> TIM: I'm just curious about how it's going with John? I notice that we seem to still be getting some hold up in the project. If I were you, I'd take him out to lunch and have a really good talk to iron out some of the issues.
>
> MIKE: Yeah, I don't think that's going to work.
>
> TIM: Hey, we just need to do whatever it takes to sort it out. Let's make it happen.

The problem lingered on. Notice what Tim did in his feedback. He started the conversation by laying out his intention: to find out what was going on with the situation with Fred, but then followed it up immediately by giving a solution to the 'problem'. The issue was, the problem was a creation of his own story. In fact, the real issue, when they finally got to the root of it, was that John's *boss* was having issues with Tim. Delivering a premature solution during feedback can tear away at trust between you and the person receiving feedback.

Tip 3: Assume good intentions

One of the things that can really help lubricate the Collaborative Feedback conversation is assuming good intention. What do I mean by this? Simply assume unproductive behaviours were done with a good intention. It can help build another layer of safety and invite people into the conversation. Here are a few examples I've heard:

- 'I can see that you are trying your hardest, but I notice that you don't seem to be getting the results you want.'
- 'I notice there was conflict in the room although I'm sure that it was innocent. Did you realize that as he raised his tone, your volume got louder and louder and you began to throw in comments that could be construed as take it or leave it?'
- 'One of your staff told me that you had raised your voice at her. I'm sure there must be lots of factors involved... but...'
- 'I noticed you didn't follow the plan we had agreed on. I'm sure there were extenuating circumstances that I'm not aware of so I'd just like to understand your thinking...'
- 'I notice your room still isn't tidy – I'm sure you had every intention to do it, can I just enquire why not?'

Just assume that the person had a good and noble reason. I personally believe that most of the time, people have the best of intentions, but sometimes other factors cause them to act otherwise. They are trying to do their best with the situation they are in. Ascribing good intention makes a big difference in the lubrication of the conversation.

Tip 4: Feedbacking on the feedback you get

Sometimes, you may have to give feedback on the feedback you get. This happens most often when the answer to your initial feedback doesn't seem to be connected (in your mind) to the conversation you think you are starting. This happens more often than you think as people commonly fail to follow the thread of the conversation. When this happens, you can use the Preparation Tool to get the conversation back on track.

Here's an example a little while back as I was facilitating a meeting:

> ME: Can I just interrupt for a second to bring something up? Maybe it's just me and my limited understanding, but I notice the conversation seems to be going round and round in circles with people changing the subject from time to time, without any conclusions being made. I think if this continues, we won't have made the decisions we need to make in the time we have available. What do you think?
>
> TEAM MEMBER: Yeah, this always happens. But can I just add to my last point I was making—
>
> ME: Sorry for interrupting again. I'm sure your point is important. But before you make it, can I just get some clarification on the current conversation we are having? I brought up an issue about meeting dynamics and posed a question to the group, and then I noticed the subject seemed to change back to the one before – without

responding to the issue I had raised. I might have read the situation wrongly, but am I missing something?

TEAM MEMBER: Oh, sorry. I didn't realize I was doing that.

Sometimes you may have to patiently and skilfully keep doing this to keep a conversation on track.

Tip 5: Tone and body language

Finally, I'd like to mention vocal tone and body language – which I covered in a previous chapter but is worth restating again. Your tone and body language play a huge part in the overall message you are trying to communicate. Indeed, if your tones and body language seem to be sending a different message to the words you are saying, people will tend to believe the former.

If you feel like the feedback is very tricky, please, please pay particular attention to your tone of voice. Most household arguments are driven by tone not by the content. If you've ever wondered why you are in an argument for no apparent reason, more than likely one party has injected a 'rogue' tone that isn't picked up consciously, wreaking havoc with our communication processes. Can it really be that important whether the toilet seat is up or down or is it something else that is at play? I have a theory about this. There are two factors at play:

1. Throughout life, we have been conditioned (called 'conditioning'[2] which refers to stimulus and response). All of us, at some point, have had unpleasant experiences from reprimands and arguments (and even worse) –

from parents, teachers, older siblings, friends, authority figures. These experiences are associated with shouting, aggressive whispers, changes in tones, changes in body language, and we have learned to react to them. Our reactions are now subconsciously automatic. So, it's not necessarily the content we are responding to; it's the conditioning to the tone of voice and changes in body language.

2. This is coupled with an inbuilt evolutionary response to threat and changes in our environment. When animals exhibit aggression or fear, there are changes in their physiology. For instance, it's well documented that when hippos repeatedly yawn, people assume the animal is happy and content. The yawns are, in fact, a threat sign. I've noticed when people are apprehensive about bringing up tricky content, sometimes there is a small perceptible yawn. It's signs like this and other subtle cues that kick our evolutionary defence systems into play. Our bodies, whether we're aware of it or not are continually scanning the environment for changes that signify threat. (if you want to know more read: *Dominance and Aggression in Humans and Other Animals – The Great Game of Life* by Henry R. Hermann).

In my experience, most people aren't very skilled at keeping their vocal tones under control, nor are they aware of the factors that drive their tone and body language. A couple of months ago, I was watching several family videos with my kids. As I watched, I was shocked by the tones I used to interact with my children because I consider myself to be laid back and pleasant in my parenting. In my work with managers and organizations, I notice tones change automatically, systematically and unconsciously as managers interact with those 'lower' than them in the hierarchy. If you're a manager and you videoed all your tonal interactions, I'm pretty sure you'd be shocked too.

One of the things that will help you maintain non-aggressive tones is getting into the right kinds of states and maintaining curiosity, as I described earlier. What will also help is focusing on it's simply your story. If you focus on this, it will help keep your tones and body language appropriate.

Be aware of your tone and body language because it will pay dividends for your feedback conversations.

I hope this chapter has helped you to feel more confident in having Collaborative Feedback conversations.

Recap

- Establish your own routine to get into the right kind of state to give feedback.
- Open the adjustment feedback conversation using the three principles of offer, outcome and outlook.
- Pay particular attention to building safety. You may find yourself having to do this again and again throughout the conversation. You do this by referring to the outcome, communicating it's only your story and making sure the person feels heard.
- Be aware of the power dynamic, which especially reveals itself through vocal tone and body language.
- Be aware when you label people as 'prickly' or 'sensitive'. If you do, take extra care to prepare your feedback.
- When giving feedback, be careful not to jump in with the solution before you've jointly agreed on the problem.
- Assuming undesirable behaviour comes from a place of good intention can help the feedback conversation to go smoothly,
- Feedback can be an iterative process. Don't be afraid of repeating yourself to get clarity. Remember it's a dance.
- Pay particular attention to your tone and body language; they usually reside out of conscious awareness.

CHAPTER 7

UTILIZING THE POWER OF AFFIRMATIONAL FEEDBACK

I'm particularly excited to be covering this chapter – I really am. When I see affirmational feedback used to its full potential, it's powerful. It can make an enormous difference to work culture; it can make an enormous impact on the lives of individuals and adds creative energy. When I talk about affirmational feedback, I'm referring to much more than simply praise or a recognition of a job well done. And so long as it's done in a spirit of sincerity and authenticity, it's a win for everyone.

Unlike adjustment feedback, there isn't a lot that can go wrong with affirmational feedback – after all, you're only communicating they are doing a great job – more of the same, please. Good stuff!

The issue with affirmational feedback, however, is, that there isn't enough of it and when it is present, it's often not done in such a way that maximizes its power.

Affirmational feedback can also be collaborative – it tends not to be, especially here in the UK. When someone compliments us with a job well done, we tend to brush it off as if it were nothing but walk away, secretly pleased. But imagine if you took that opportunity to get collaborative? What better time to open a feedback conversation, than when all your strengths are in the foreground? More about this later.

There are many benefits to utilizing the power of affirmational feedback. Organizations are forever looking for ways to motivate their staff and look at their reward systems regularly to see what can be improved. They look to see what can be incentivized, bonuses and such like, promotional opportunities, but these all come at a cost. And sometimes the opportunities are just not there, or they are there, but not right now.

What is continuously overlooked is working at a culture of affirmation. When affirmational feedback is done right, it can stay with an individual and/or teams for the rest of their careers. You can probably still remember, all those years ago, when one of your teachers gave you some uplifting feedback. Didn't it have an impact on your life? Encouraged you to do even more? You may have even embarked upon a different career as a result.

The benefits of affirmational feedback are huge, and it doesn't cost anything except a bit of forethought and a few seconds to let someone know they are doing great!

One of the things I do regularly with my program participants is to ask them when was the last time they received some 'positive' feedback. Their answers, way too often, are the same – not recently, not enough and not meaningful enough.

When affirmational feedback is given on a regular and thoughtful basis, they report it makes a tremendous difference in their colleagues' lives and their own. Imagine if it were a regular occurrence in your workplace. How encouraging would it be to work there? How much more motivational for everyone? How much more creativity and motion?

Also, when affirmational feedback is given well, it allows people to have insights into their own development and informs best practices for organizations.

Greg missed the opportunity to open a world of possibilities by giving quality, affirmational feedback.

Some of the benefits of giving affirmational feedback are listed below:

- It encourages people to keep going.
- It builds trust.
- It lifts the mood of the atmosphere.
- It builds morale in the workforce.
- Increases capabilities in the organization.
- It extracts best practice.
- It is beneficial for your wellbeing – it feels great to be the bearer of good news.
- It's a development tool.

How to unleash the power of affirmational feedback

Here are my insights for giving affirmational feedback that makes a difference to people:

- Be sincere.
- Do it with an attitude of appreciation and not necessarily praise.
- Get super specific with the details.
- Prepare it like you would adjustment feedback.

Be sincere

First, when you give affirmational feedback, be really sincere – and that's actually really easy. When you truly look at what people are doing, it's incredible. Karen, my wife, has a habit of continually reminding me of the beauty of nature. She'll say, 'Come over here, honey, and look at the sunset, sunrise, the trees, the birds eating away at the food that we left for them, the scenery, the mountains, the valleys, the blue sky and so on.' And when you take time to just pause and take in what is in front of you, you begin to feel reverence and awe.

But get this: you can do it with any person too. People are amazing. They are intricate, sophisticated, complex; millions of neuronal processes taking place at any time, the body regulating itself – even how they stand, balance, walk, talk to one another is amazing. When you take a second to get into that zone, you begin to feel a real appreciation of the miracle of a human being in front of you. Then it becomes easy to get sincere about the affirmational feedback you are about to give. The trick is to slow down your thinking and gain awareness of what's around you.

One of the things I often harp on about in my work with senior teams and managers is the art of slowing down in their thinking. I see a trend of businesses operating faster and faster, trying to keep up with the enormous changes that are happening technologically and globally. I see key decisions being made with inadequate examination and reflection of data, that in turn generates frantic activity for everyone. The question is, does that activity add any more value to the business? The answer to that, is sadly, all too often, not.

Slow down your thinking when it comes to people and notice what's around you. When you do, you'll see things that you haven't seen before, get insights that are waiting for you to be discovered and realize the brilliance of people. Then you can give your affirmational feedback from that place of genuine sincerity.

Do it with an attitude of appreciation and not necessarily praise

Don't get me wrong – it's not necessarily wrong to praise. I really loved the work that Ken Blanchard and Spencer Johnson did on the *One Minute Manager* all those years ago. Everyone loves a bit of genuine praise. If you want to give praise, please do so. Praise, however, has a power connotation connected with it. It's an 'I am in a position to give you praise' type situation. A parent praises their child; a superior praises those who are inferior. If what we are trying to do is to give everyone a sense of ownership and a sense of true collaboration, I believe that sometimes subtly, praise works against these things. Also, it doesn't necessarily work both ways. It's appropriate for your boss to give you praise, but it isn't necessarily appropriate for you to give praise to your boss. Can you imagine saying, 'Well done for managing me!'

What works much better in my opinion, is the articulation of appreciation for a skilful execution of a job well done. It's always appropriate to appreciate.

It's physically and emotionally good for the giver to dish out appreciative, affirmational feedback and it's super encouraging for the receiver to get. Your organization needs this to be resilient, sustainable and adaptable. Everyone knows it's good to be appreciative, and we all like to be appreciated for the efforts we contribute.

Infuse your affirmational feedback with the energy of appreciation. Your colleagues will love and thank you for it.

Get super specific on the details

This is where you can make the real difference in your affirmational feedback – the more specific, the better. I ask people what kinds of things are said when they receive 'affirmational feedback. The most common answers are things like:

- 'Good job.'
- 'Well done.'
- 'That was great.'
- 'You did a fabulous job.'
- 'Brilliant.'
- 'That was excellent – keep going.'

These words are encouraging, but they could be so much more impactful.

One of the lessons I learned earlier on in marriage was in the art of apologizing. 'What's this got to do with affirmational feedback?' I hear you ask. Hold on – I'm getting there. When I did something wrong, I would simply say, 'Sorry love' or 'sorry darling' to which my wife would regularly reply, 'For what exactly?' Here's one of my rare moments of semi-enlightenment in an incident that happened a couple of decades ago. Once again, it has to do with the tidiness of our house. I use this illustration, as I know it's not just in our household that these opportunities for feedback occur.

KAREN: Sigh! [*Disappointed look on her face.*]

CHRIS: That's a heavy sigh.

KAREN: The house is so messy, and you said you'd help tidy it up.

CHRIS: Yeah, sorry about that.

KAREN: Is that it?

CHRIS: Err, is there more? I'll do it now.

KAREN: What are you sorry for?

CHRIS: For not tidying the house when I said I would?

KAREN: I'm really upset... And I don't think you understand.

CHRIS: What do you want me to say?

KAREN: I just need to know that you understand.

CHRIS: What? What?

KAREN: Well, if you don't get it, you don't get it.

CHRIS: What do you want me to say? That you've been out working hard all day with a million things to do on your list, which is stressful, that your stress was compounded because your parents are coming over later – and you hate the house being untidy when they do. And then, to top it all, I promised to help, and you were really hoping that I was going to keep my promise, even though my past record isn't the best, and your hopes were dashed again, and you feel really disappointed? Is that what you want me to say?

KAREN: Thank you. Now get off your butt and help me sort out the house.

That incident stayed with me because I had an insight that has helped our communication and our marriage ever since – It wasn't until I got specific about my actions and thinking did my wife know and feel, that I saw the error of my ways; and that my sorry really was a genuine sorry!

In the same way, people can see a real genuineness in your affirmational feedback when you get specific in your appreciation or praise. Communicate what you noticed in their actions and behaviour and lay your thinking on the table. It's about empathy and showing a real understanding of what the person did. When you see and understand what they are doing, and are capable of, inside, they'll respond with a 'Wow, you get me!' And here's the really encouraging bit. Sometimes people can't even see their own brilliance – and when you shine a light on it and help reveal what's hidden, it brings a level of encouragement that is deep – way deep.

In my training, when people begin to really apply specificity to their affirmational feedback, they report back that it makes a massive difference and adds a dimension to relationships they had not known was there.

So how do you get specific? First, decide to be a better observer. Really look and think about what people do, how they do it and even the order in which they do it.

Once again, the Collaborative Feedback Preparation Tool we explored in Chapter 5 comes in handy, albeit the slightly abbreviated version. When you run the preparation tool, it gives you great material in which to choose to give your affirmational feedback. Below is the abbreviated Feedback Tool:

1. My outcome is...
2. What I notice is...
3. The meaning I make of this is...

Here's an example that one of my program participants shared. The situation was a manager giving feedback to one of her team members, an account manager who was managing a difficult client who kept changing the parameters of the project.

My outcome is I really want her to see how much I am in awe of her skills in this area.

What I notice is she summarized the flow of the conversation four times; she made sure she framed the conversation considering the previous meeting; she asked six questions and injected humour on several occasions.

The meaning I make of this is that by summarizing and asking the questions, she got clarity and understanding with the client that wouldn't have been there. By framing the conversation considering the previous meeting, she made sure the client was reminded of earlier promises, and by injecting humour, she made the experience a pleasant one for all.

When she gave the feedback, it went like this:

MANAGER: Hey, can I just say what a fantastic job you did with the client last week?

ACCOUNT MANAGER: Thank you.

MANAGER: I was so in awe of the way you handled it. You summarized the flow on at least four occasions and asked questions at the appropriate time to get real clarity – something we haven't been able to get before. You made sure that the client was reminded of previous promises, and you did it with a wicked sense of humour that caught the client off guard. That was so skilfully done.

ACCOUNT MANAGER: I did all that?

MANAGER: Yeah that's what I saw

ACCOUNT MANAGER: Wow. Thank you. Thank you so much for sharing that.

The manager shared with me how impacting the feedback was to the account manager and how satisfying it was to give it. Oh, the joy of being a bearer of good news!

The abbreviated affirmational Feedback Tool

Let's take a closer look at how to use the abbreviated tool and break it down step by step.

My outcome is...

Why would you need to choose an outcome when you are giving affirmational feedback? In the case of adjustment feedback, you want to check that you are giving it for the right reasons, that it connects to something tangible and that you have a chance of it turning into a collaborative conversation.

With affirmational feedback, you can use the sentence starter to strategically plan how you want the effects of the feedback to go. It enables you to frame the feedback and choose the language and examples you want the recipient to embrace. Below are examples of a few:

- My outcome is to help him see how he is progressing in his relationships with his team.
- My outcome is to make her aware of how resourceful she is.
- My outcome is to help him see how well rounded he is and how that benefits everyone else.
- My outcome is to help my manager feel how appreciative I am for the way she manages me and how it really helps me.
- My outcome is to help him take even more control of his own development.

Note: the last one is a combination of both adjustment and affirmational feedback.

Notice the amount of creative scope you have, as the same behaviour can mean so many things. Let's imagine you want to give an employee some affirmational feedback. You notice she always has a bright smile for everyone. You can frame the feedback in so many ways. What does that smile mean and how does it have a positive impact?

- Your smile is infectious and brings positive energy to your whole team.
- Your smile communicates you are so appreciative of people. What a wonderful trait!

- Your smile makes people want to work with you, and that's what makes you effective in your role.

Even if the behaviours you notice are the same, you can still frame it differently to focus on the areas you want to focus on. That's why it's useful to focus on the outcome.

I notice...

Again, stick to things you have heard or seen or can hear and/or can see. One of the things that can help you here is to take sequences of things you have heard or seen into account because it's often the sequence that makes what you've seen special and skilful.

When you pay attention to specific things you have seen or heard and take the sequencing into account, you are executing the first steps of business-skill modelling. You are mapping a set of intricate skills that makes an individual effective. Those of you who are familiar with NLP (neuro-linguistic programming) modelling will know exactly what I'm talking about.

What are the things they do, that make them effective or excellent? Below are a few examples:

- I noticed that she physically handed the client the prospectus to touch and experience as part of the sales routine.
- I noticed he used a sequence of questions, punctuated by statements so as not to make the conversation sound like an interrogation.
- I noticed he stayed until 9 p.m. to work on your presentation and ran it through from start to finish eight times.

- I noticed in her presentation that her vocal tone subtly changed to communicate the importance of a part of the content.
- I notice that when you are in danger of missing a deadline, you always flag up the risk at least a week before.
- I notice you take time to have an interaction with everyone in your department every day.
- I noticed that as the tone and volume of her voice rose in frustration, she didn't respond likewise and I also noticed that brought the tension in the conversation back under control
- I notice she always starts her verbal updates with context right up front and then asks a question to ensure the other person has really heard her.

And the list can go on and on… the more you notice, the more resources you will have to feed into your affirmational feedback conversation. It's what you can actually see or hear that makes the difference.

As a youngster at school, I always believed I was rubbish at art. What I drew looked nothing like real life. But then I read a book called *Drawing on the Right Side* of the Brain by Betty Edwards. It opened my eyes as to why I thought I was 'bad' at art. It turns out that the quality of how we do art depends mainly on what we can see and what we cannot.

When most 'non-artists' draw what is in front of them, they actually don't see what is in front of them, they are actually reproducing on paper a mental picture of what they think is in front of them. And their mental picture is often a distorted one. For example, if I think a nose is shaped like a curved 'L' shape then I will tend to draw it like that – even though it looks nothing like that on the person in front of me.

Artists see differently. They process information in terms of basic shapes, relationships between lines, shades of colours, empty space, and so on. The ordinary person sees a nose or a mouth or an ear.

When we really learn to break down what we see and hear and map them usefully, it's a tremendously useful skill on which to develop capability and processes that are unique to our organizations and that adds tremendous value.

And the meaning I make of that is...

This is where you can get creative and really magnify the effect of your affirmational feedback. When we take what we notice, we can attach any meaning to it we like, so long as we are creative enough to make the links. This makes our affirmational feedback unique, well thought through, distinctive and special. This stops the clichéd efforts which people roll their eyes at. Let's take some of the examples above and play with the meaning a little bit and see what we can get:

- I noticed that she handed the client the prospectus as part of the sales routine – and that means she has an in-depth understanding of sales psychology.
- I noticed that he used a sequence of questions, punctuated by statements so as not to make the conversation sound like an interrogation – and that means he's very astute and alert to conversational nuances which make a big difference.

- I noticed he stayed until 9 p.m. to work on his presentation and ran it through from start to finish eight times and that means he demonstrates an unusual drive and an approach to mastery that's rare to see.
- I notice that when you are in danger of missing a deadline, you always flag up the risk at least a week before and that means you have a critical business instinct for spotting risks and managing potential fallout.

Get the idea? When you put meaning on what you notice, it generates a depth of real appreciation. It's a highly creative process. Let's do one more, but this time let's play with it to demonstrate how one set of observations can mean many different things, so that your affirmational feedback may forever continue to show a ton of variety.

- I notice you take time to have an interaction with everyone in your department every day, **and that means** you can connect with anyone – such a powerful business skill.
- I notice you take time to have an interaction with everyone in your department every day, **and that means** you have the uncanny ability to focus in on the long-term growth and development of your team.
- I notice you take time to have an interaction with everyone in your department every day, **and that means** you put a real emphasis on the lives of your co-workers.

- I notice you take time to have an interaction with everyone in your department every day, **and that means** you are such an encouraging person.
- I notice you take time to have an interaction with everyone in your department every day, **and that means** you are the glue of the entire team.
- I notice you take time to have an interaction with everyone in your department every day, **and that means** you have an amazing consistency to focus on the heart of the organization – the people.
- I notice you take time to have an interaction with everyone in your department every day, **and that means** you have a real appreciation for what it means to be human.

You get the idea? The list is endless and is only limited by how creative you can get.

One participant on the program decided to give some affirmational feedback to her director, who was two or three levels higher than her in the organization and who she had very little interaction with daily. She managed to grab him in the cafeteria to give some affirmational feedback.

> PROGRAM PARTICIPANT: Can I just take a second to thank you for your leadership. I notice that decisions escalated to you consistently get resolved in less than a week – that makes the team feel secure and we're not left hanging. I've worked for other leaders who don't get this.
>
> DIRECTOR: Thank you. That's very kind of you to say that
>
> PROGRAM PARTICIPANT: Not at all

The participant told me how that interaction had impacted her, how it had empowered her and somehow lowered the power differential between the two. When she saw how her director reacted to the feedback (genuinely surprised and pleased), she realized she could influence people who she deemed to be beyond her sphere of influence.

Affirmational feedback and development

I believe that affirmational feedback done in such a way can play a big part in the development of people. One popular and influential model, 'The Kolb Learning Cycle', postulates that we learn by going through a cycle. We have an experience; we reflect on it; we make meaning of it and then experiment and/or act on our conceptualization.

Affirmational feedback can play a significant role in two aspects of this cycle. First, it encourages people to reflect. Reflection only happens on data and/or information of which you are conscious. There are lots of things that people do and say that stay out of their consciousness, and you can play a pivotal role in bringing this data to light. You can also play a role in helping shape meaning from their experience and thereby mould and accelerate their learning.

Affirmational feedback also helps to embed desirable behaviours in the organization. From time to time, we run a sales program and get participants to sign up to affirmational feedback to embed the sales behaviours they are looking for. When you get specific about what people are doing well, they want to do more of it and quickly because it's a powerful way of changing habits.

Finally, in this section, I'd like to share how affirmational feedback can be a fantastic foundation for revealing best practice. If employees are continually looking for see/hear behaviours, patterns of behaviour; sequences of events and their consequences, they kick into a type of learning and adjusting that makes clear best practices. If you're a manager, you'll know that processes and strategies look all well and good on paper, but it's not until you do it, that you begin to see what works and what doesn't. With the mindset that comes with affirmational feedback, you begin to more clearly see what's effective and what isn't. Make these explicit and compare them with other alternative processes, and soon you'll emerge with best practice.

I hope from this chapter that you'll take time to transform your affirmational feedback into something that deeply touches the hearts of your colleagues. Use the abbreviated Preparation Tool to make it come to life. Just make sure it's real and sincere, and you'll see the difference it will make to you and to others over time.

Finally, a quick word to say that people do amazing things at work. They should be thanked and appreciated for what they do. It's the appropriate thing to do for our businesses and for our lives. Affirmational feedback: Do it better and do it more! Feedback is a gift, especially affirmational feedback. It's a joy to give gifts, and they can be in constant supply.

Recap

- Affirmational feedback can make an enormous difference to the people you give it to.
- The benefits of affirmational feedback are huge, and it doesn't cost anything except a bit of forethought and a few seconds of your time.
- When giving affirmational feedback, remember to:
- Be sincere.
- Do it with an attitude of appreciation and not praise.
- Get super specific with details.
- Get creative with attaching meaning to the positive behaviours you notice.
- Use the abbreviated Feedback Tool to help you prepare affirmational feedback.
- Use affirmational feedback to turn the conversation into a coaching conversation that embeds capabilities and best practice.
- Affirmational feedback helps with individual and team development.
- Affirmational feedback is a gift. Give freely and give thoughtfully.

CHAPTER 8

THE CREATIVE ART OF RECEIVING FEEDBACK

In my travels in the corporate world, I hear people talk about how important it is to be able to learn the skill of giving feedback and holding difficult conversations. Very rarely do I hear about another skill; one that's just as important, and that would affect the organizational culture profoundly – receiving feedback. If you've ever been at the receiving end of poorly delivered adjustment feedback and reacted badly, then this chapter is for you. Even if you've been lucky and never experienced poorly delivered feedback, there's a good chance you might find some nuggets that will help you to process the feedback you get more effectively.

As I described in the introduction, in my younger days, when someone gave me 'negative' feedback, I would simply stand there with a glazed look on my face. My mind would turn to mush, thoughts would scramble, and if someone asked me what I thought of the feedback, I would simply shake my head and shrug my shoulders, or I would make up some things to say that I thought might please them. I would then feel stupid, shallow and spend an inordinate amount of time berating myself. Then I would move on to the next phase and proceed, in my mind, to have a go at the feedback giver for sending me down that uncomfortable cycle.

Later, I adopted a slightly different strategy. I was still dazed, my mind still scrambled, but if they asked me what I thought, I simply replied, 'I need time to process it. I'm the reflective type. Let me get back to you.' That felt much better.

To some extent, this served me well, but it meant that I missed benefitting from the feedback because, as you now know, quality feedback is a collaborative process; a combination of your perspective and theirs – that's where the value lies. Oh, and I still felt a bit stupid. I had just learned to fake it better. I hadn't learned how to process feedback or realized it was a skill I could acquire.

I've seen so many incidences where people don't process feedback skilfully and are crushed by it as a result. We've all heard of instances where dreams and talents are wiped away because of a feedback comment gone wrong. Think of stories you've heard about the teacher who said the wrong thing and ruined the dreams of the child. We must help people learn to process challenging feedback in a way that is useful to them – in a way that helps them grow.

Fatima froze whenever someone gave her challenging feedback because she didn't have an effective way of processing it.

In organizations many undesirable things happen when people are unskilled at processing feedback. In fact, it can wreak havoc. I remember having a conversation with a manager who was feeling hugely stressed because she had been accused of bullying by someone she managed, and who had taken out a grievance against her for inappropriate comments. Her manager, the HR director, was also stressed because he relied on this manager, and she was taking time off for stress. The main crux of the problem seemed to be in a couple of conversations, the manager had used some poorly chosen words. This had then been misinterpreted by the recipient, and things spiralled. If the manager had chosen different words or if the recipient had processed the feedback differently, all the problems could have been avoided. As I described earlier in the book, generalized language can be a minefield, especially in environments where political correctness is taken seriously.

The importance of taking control of your feedback

It is super important that you take control of the feedback you get and that you process it skilfully. How you receive feedback will impact your life, in ways you may not have considered until now. If you don't take control of feedback, you may find yourself on the receiving end of stories that are untrue, unfair or unhelpful! It may come as a surprise to you, but feedback is always in your control – even if it's delivered very unskilfully or with an inappropriate attitude by someone else. The power of feedback, either good or bad, lies in the story that is created from the information that is given. Stories are simply stories and, whether you know it or not, you have the power to control them any time you want. You can always break feedback down into something useful for you and in the process, build and influence your relationship with the giver.

It may come as a surprise to you, but feedback is always in your control as the receiver.

The deeper picture: Beliefs and values

Before we begin looking at how to skilfully process feedback, let's take a slightly deeper dive into the way we operate as human beings – in particular, how, we, as humans, are intrinsic storytellers and how these stories affect our lives in very real ways. This will help us gain awareness in the way we process our feedback. And when we are more aware, we are more able to mould the feedback in a way that serves us. Somehow, just knowing that we are constructing these stories and understanding how they are constructed, is enough for us to be able to construct different, more helpful stories.

We continually generate stories about ourselves, others and the world at large – it's part of what it means to be human. We need these stories to learn so that we can navigate our environment 'safely' and 'effectively'. We make up stories as to what is appropriate or inappropriate, what is possible or not possible. These stories benefit us, hinder us and affect how we interact with everything. We often don't fully realize the power these stories hold or even know they are there most of the time, yet they affect all our behaviours, our moods, and how we experience life in general. We hold intricate stories about ourselves, our identities and attach expectations to these stories. When others try and change these stories without our permission, we experience inner friction – we can resist, defend ourselves, be hurt, confused or even devastated.

There are two different categories of stories that we create and tell ourselves that are important for feedback – belief stories and value stories. Let's explore these:

The belief story

We create, tell and store stories in our bodies about what things are and how they work in our world – our beliefs. There are three types of belief stories:

- Definition stories
- Causation stories
- Possibility stories

Definition stories primarily talk about 'what *means* what' – our inner model of how we define things. Causation stories tell us about 'what *causes* what' – our inner models of cause and effect. Possibility stories tell us about what's possible and what's not.

Definition stories play an intricate part of our human experience: my boss is good, my director is bad, my daughter is clever, my son is athletic, collaboration is good, competition is bad, I am good, I am kind, I am worthless, I am awesome – all these are examples of definition stories. Notice the words 'is' and 'am' because they form some sort of equivalence. Also, notice how the latter two examples are identity statements. Identity statements hold extraordinary power over us. More about these later.

Causation stories are our mind's attempts to predict what might happen next. Investing in this area leads to more opportunity or less opportunity; hard work leads to success; feedback leads to learning; good leadership leads to successful organizations – all these are examples of causation stories – what causes what.

Possibility stories let us know what's possible, thereby helping us to avoid wasting time on activities that will lead to failure. 'I can win this race,' 'I can't do presentations well,' 'I can manage large groups of people,' 'I can't get on with my boss' are all examples of possibility stories and have the power to release or limit our potential.

These three story types play a huge part in driving our behaviours. For example, if we think Johan is evil, we'll tend to avoid him, and if we think Stephanie is encouraging, we might look to hang out with her. If we don't think we can get the promotion, we don't go after it, and if I'm not the kind of person who likes selling, I avoid selling. So, here's how knowing this can help – when receiving feedback, pay attention to the belief stories you are constructing and question them:

- Does the rise of the eyebrow mean that they are disrespecting you?
- Does the fact that you have had a disciplinary mean you won't be promoted anytime soon?
- Does the fact that you've found it hard to talk to your mother for many years mean that you will never talk to her easily?
- Does the fact that you generate activity mean you are making progress?
- Does 15 'failures' mean you aren't going to be great at sales?

- Does asking for advice mean you are weak?
- Does having a new car mean you are more successful?
- Does never having money mean it's hard to generate income in the future?
- Does not having your pension sorted now, mean you will suffer hard times?
- Does hard work lead to success?
- Does hiring the most talented people cause the organization to be successful?
- Does challenging your boss really cause you to be seen as disloyal?

These are all types of stories that we may construct. They are hardly ever true per se. They only feel like they are.

You see, once a story is constructed and you confirm it with an inner 'yes', it starts having power over you. You tend to take it as truth, your body begins to internalize it and, very shortly after, you won't even remember you've constructed the story. You'll just know it's true inside your body – and it will affect how you think and behave. To compound it even further, once this happens, then we have a mechanism inside of us called the 'reticular activation system' that looks for evidence to prove that our story is true and reinforces it.[3] That's how beliefs work.

A special kind of belief story – our identity stories

There's a special kind of definition story that particularly affects us in the way we receive feedback. These are stories we've created about who we are at our core – our identity story. Our identity stories have a particular structure to them. It's the 'I am…' structure. Here are some examples:

- I am kind.
- I am weak.
- I am a loser.
- I am a mother.
- I am funny.
- I am not funny.
- I am confident.
- I am not confident.
- I am detailed.
- I am selfish.
- I am fun.
- I am a leader.
- I am a follower.
- I am honest.
- I am not a hypocrite.

Some of these can be helpful, but others aren't. And what you'll find is, in some contexts what is helpful won't be helpful and vice-versa. And the stronger you feel and believe these types of statements are the truth about you, the more powerful they are.

There are a couple of issues with identity stories that may be worth examining in the light of feedback:

1. We can prematurely and inappropriately turn experiences into 'negative' identity statements, which then cause limitation stories. These stop us from fulfilling our potential and cause us problems because our bodies and minds react to them. We can then generalize even further. Some people seem to do this as a matter of habit. These are the people who we may label as 'prickly'.
    - 'You didn't draw that very accurately' can become 'I am not an artist.'
    - 'You hurt her feelings' can become 'I am not good with people.'
    - 'You could have done better' can become 'See I told you, I am unlikeable.'
    - 'I don't understand what you are saying' can become 'I am someone who nobody gets. I am alone.'
2. When we come across information (in feedback) that seems to conflict with our identity statements, we experience a deep inner discomfort that often stops us in our tracks. Our bodies and minds react to them. It may cause us to defend our corner, run away from the conversation or just send us into a daze. The need to defend our identity becomes more important than finding help in the feedback.

You can see how some of these identity stories can be very destructive and drive all sorts of strange and unwanted behaviours.

When we become aware of our identity stories, and how we create them, we can consciously affect their construction – thereby negating some of the unwanted emotion, while we take on board feedback.

Also, realize that your identity statements are psychological constructs. Are they true? Who knows? If you believe they're true, they'll feel like they're true.

In the West, we hold a story about identity that seems to be widespread. This story says something like – we have a true identity that is the real us. Find it, live according to it, and you will find authenticity and happiness. This 'bigger' story about the way we hold identity can cause people problems when they don't live in accordance to what they think of as their 'true self', or when they feel they are unable to find it. It can also cause limitation issues, such as 'I'm not that type of person, so I can't do that!'

There are other stories or psychological constructs we can tell ourselves about our identities, which you may not have come across and might be useful.

One story about identity that I've found to be useful in recent times is the story of what's really behind our 'apparent' identities – thought. Clare Dimond, in her book, *Real. The Inside Out Guide to Being Yourself* says:

...Our idea of a self isn't a true self. Our idea of who we are is a compilation of changing thoughts and beliefs. Who we think we are is not who we are, never was and never will be. Deep down we know this. We know that everything we think about who we are can flip to the opposite thought in a heartbeat. One minute we think we are a loser. The next minute we think we are doing OK. One moment, we think we are kind. The next moment, we are nasty. One moment, it looks like people love and respect us. The next we seem like an outcast.

...What if we realised that 24 hours a day, thought is flowing through our minds. Some of that thought we will notice, believe, act on and, from that, an apparent reality is created. When we see that the content of thought is fluid, ever-changing and transient, it has far less validity or gravitas.

It's only your thoughts ever that is creating the emotion, not the reality.

The value story

Another type of story we construct is value stories. These are stories that we create about what is important and what isn't. Below are a few examples of these:

- It's important to get ahead in your career.
- It's important to set yourself up for your future life.
- It's important to be tidy.
- It's important to always be on time.
- It's important to keep everyone happy.
- It's important to buy an expensive watch.
- It's important to be seen to be fashionable.

These stories are linked intrinsically with our belief, identity and possibility stories; they are an interconnected mesh. Often you can predict someone's value stories from their belief stories and vice-versa. So, for example, 'being successful at my job means my mother will accept me' might become 'being successful at my job is more important than spending time with my children'.

We also tend to take these stories further by creating stories about our value stories. For example, we might create a story about what it means to be tidy. My wife has a very useful (albeit sometimes inconvenient for me) story that she tells about tidiness: 'Everything must have a proper place in our house.' Other people tell themselves a story about what it means to be successful. 'I must get to the very top of the tree' to be successful' – even if the process in doing so, causes deep unhappiness.

I remember having a boss when I was just out of university who reprimanded me for being late. I looked at my watch and said, 'But I'm on time?' He responded, 'Being on time is getting here five minutes early!' (Or... is it?)

The issue with value stories is when someone seems to display thinking or behaviour that contradicts your value stories, we tend to feel hurt or decide they are not the type of person we like or get on with. This has massive implications for diversity, for developing an inclusive work culture or even inclusive societies.

But once again, value stories are simply stories that we have created at one time or other. If when processing feedback, we are aware of how it runs into our value stories, it will help us to process feedback more usefully. It might also help you to realize – if you can stomach this – that anytime you feel hurt by someone, it's because they have stepped on your self-created values – so in some ways, you've been instrumental in hurting yourself. Radical I know but if truly taken on board, that line of thinking will take you away from a victim mentality. You might need to reflect on this one.

Pay attention to your belief stories, identity stories and value stories as you process feedback! OK – now we've got that as a background, let's move on to how we can join the collaborative party as the receiver of feedback.

How to receive feedback collaboratively

First, remember that Collaborative Feedback isn't a one-way process. It's a two-way (or more) thing. It's a collaboration so that we can learn and take things forward. Seek an opportunity as early as possible to join the party. Add to the creative process. It will stop you from feeling like you are on the back foot and having to defend or run away from the feedback.

Appreciate the feedback – see it as a gift always

Appreciate the feedback you are getting. Feedback is always a gift if you choose to accept it as such. The giver has taken time to offer you information and a perspective that can always be useful – even if it's poorly given. If you see feedback as a present or an invitation, you will always gain something useful. If you want, thank them for the information they are offering.

Don't forget their feedback says just as much about them as it does about you, so in that sense, it is personal – but in this case, to them, not you. Remember, in an earlier chapter when I described how – to give personal feedback – the giver must first construct a story inside their head. It's just as much about their beliefs, their values and their standards as it is about the truth or reality of what's really happening. Understanding this will help you to not take it personally, and additionally, you'll also learn something about them, which may help you to further build that relationship.

I remember giving my older brother feedback many years ago about pulling his weight in the house when he came home from university. In fact, I think I went on a rant. I remember him looking at me strangely as if to say, 'What the hell are you talking about?' Then he said, 'Don't make your story, my story!' I'll always remember that.

And if you're the giver of feedback, you'll do well to remember that it is initially just your story – being aware of this will help the receiver engage.

Take ownership for any feedback given

You know you've taken ownership of your stories when you really believe that the feedback is yours to control and shape. Think of the information like a lump of clay. It may come in one form, but you warm it with your hands and turn it into something else. They are simply stories. And if you're thinking, 'Yes that all very easy to say, but sometimes these stories feel so real,' realize that the 'real feeling' is also a story that you are telling yourself. When you take ownership for your feedback, you'll also mould the story into something useful, encouraging and practical. And guess what? You can use the simple model of giving feedback to process personal feedback that you get – how convenient!

- I notice...that the feedback giver said this about me
- The meaning I choose to make of that is...
- And that might mean...

Get to the intention of the feedback

This is an important point. As we've explored earlier, people often communicate something different in their feedback than their original intention – especially if they are feeling a little stressed at the thought of giving it. I remember having a conversation with a work colleague a few years back, which went something like this.

COLLEAGUE: I just want to say, I don't feel like you're pulling your weight in the relationship.

CHRIS: Oh, really? What do you mean?

COLLEAGUE: Well I thought we had agreed that you would deliver the piece of work in a certain way.

CHRIS: Err, I'm not sure that we did agree to that.

COLLEAGUE: Well I'm disappointed that we didn't go through it together beforehand, so we could get clarity. I have the responsibility ultimately for this project and need to ensure it goes well.

CHRIS: So, what you're trying to really say is, you'd like me to run through things with you before I deliver it?

COLLEAGUE: Well, yes.

Notice what was said initially was different from the intention of what he meant to say. I could have reacted and said what I thought – which was something like, 'Screw you.' Fortunately, I didn't, and we had a good conversation – which led to clarification on standards, the building of trust and strengthened our general working relationship.

Also, some people have a habit of working out what they are saying, as they are saying it. They're not quite sure what they think, but they say it aloud anyway as feedback, and if someone chooses to explore it with them, they'll eventually get to what they really mean. Annoying, I know – but I've met quite a few people like this in my travels.

You can get to their intention by summarizing back to them what they are saying along with stating their intention and the outcome. If you have no idea of the intention, ask for it, or you can have a guess and get them to clarify. It's up to you. By doing this, you help them to clarify the reason why they are giving it in the first place. You can do it by asking the question, **'Are you saying...?'** And here follows a few real-life examples that participants on my programs have told me about:

Example 1

GIVER: We are screwing up this project.

RECEIVER: So, can I just check what you're saying? Are you saying that we're all underperforming and you're trying to help us find ways to pick up our performance?

GIVER: No. No. We're doing well in lots of areas. I'm just trying to find ways to manage the client's expectations.

Example 2

GIVER: This is not acceptable.

RECEIVER: Just checking. Are you saying what we did was wrong and drawing our attention to it?

Example 3

GIVER: You need to be more creative.

RECEIVER: Are you saying that what I did was wrong in this situation and you want to help me find alternative solutions?

GIVER: Yes. That's what I'm saying.

By pointing the focus back to the outcome of the conversation, you can help everyone to achieve their aims.

Break down generalizations to see/hear language

This is the crux of getting to the nub of processing feedback. It's a bit like getting back to the original data points. If you do this bit well, it doesn't matter how poorly someone gives feedback, you will always be able to get to the heart of what they are saying. Lay their thinking on the table and explore it, to either:

- Learn from it (by making meaning).
- Show them the assumptions they are making.
- Create new perspectives together.

If the giver can't give skilful feedback, you can take control and break it down into a form that's helpful for everyone. You lay their thinking on the table, even if they don't know how to. Just take care to build in the safety mechanisms that we've covered in previous chapters. That way you don't come across as aggressive, defensive or inappropriate. You need never fear poorly given feedback ever again.

You break down their generalized language to see/hear language by asking the following generic question?

What specifically did you see or hear that made you think...?

Here are some examples:

- What specifically did you see or hear that made you think that I might be underperforming?
- What specifically did you see or hear that led you to think that I didn't lead the project well?

- What specifically did you see or hear that makes you think I wasn't taking ownership?
- What specifically did you see or hear that makes you think that I wasn't proactive?

To avoid coming across as defensive, it's a good idea to soften the question by first inserting outcome statements before asking it. Here are some examples below:

- So that I can understand better, what exactly did you see or hear that made you think that I might be underperforming?
- So that I can get a bit more clarity, can you give me the details of what you saw or heard that made you think that?
- So that I can plan to change it, can you let me know what it was you saw or heard specifically that led you to think I am not taking ownership?

You can also use this same method to break down affirmational feedback to get specifics that you can improve upon (or if you're like me, bask in the glory that little bit longer):

- So that I can take things higher, what specifically did you see or hear about my performance that made it a job well done?
- Thank you so much for that compliment. So that I can improve even more, what exactly did you see or hear that led you to think I was brilliant?

By asking the question, you begin to fill in the pieces of data, or information, that will reveal how their story got constructed. By doing this, you also help the giver of feedback to gain insight into their hidden stories. This benefits everyone from a learning perspective.

Explore the meaning of the story laid before you

Now that you've got the sensory data their story is created from, you can begin to learn from the story – either by yourself or with the giver of feedback. You've also got the information to push back on the feedback if that is the route you choose to take. To do this, in your mind, you can question the links in their story:

- I wonder if the tone they detected indicated passion rather than frustration?
- I wonder if the KPI (key performance indicators) results you've pointed out in my performance review are more about my personal performance or the conflicting systems that are currently in place?

At the very least, you are taking responsibility and ownership for the feedback process. Even if you don't agree with their story, you have a starting point to explore how you might proceed. Alternatively, on hearing their 'fuller' story, you might conclude, that on this occasion, the feedback is off the mark and you can choose to do nothing about it.

Another thing that happens when you start guiding the feedback conversation is, you often uncover a deeper intent or a deeper perspective from the giver. As I've said previously, people can start conversations, not knowing what they are really thinking and process as they go along.

Think of receiving feedback like mining for gold: you will always find it if you dig hard and deep enough. I believe someone else's perspective is always valuable in some way. We just don't see it yet. There have been many times when I have not understood something. But later, with reflection, the insight comes, and I begin to learn and grow.

That's because feedback only takes effect when meaning is constructed, and meaning is always a story that is created. And who creates that final story? Why you, of course! So, you take ownership; create a story that's helpful to you, not one that hinders you!

Let's go back to a story that I started right at the beginning of this book. Let me refresh your memory...

I got some feedback from a boss who had delivered some poorly chosen words, which at the time hurt a lot. In trying to help me improve my performance with clients, she had used the term, 'slimy.' (In her defence, she was actually a pretty good boss generally. I think she was just having an off day! Later, she apologized profusely when she realized what she had said.)

If I had known then what I know now, I would have immediately asked, 'And what is it that you see or hear specifically that made you think 'slimy?' Doing that would have retrieved the missing information on her unfortunate label. As it was, I didn't ask the question and went away... and cried a bit and... complained a lot to my wife... and cursed a lot... and mentally devised some ways to swiftly dispatch her... and then eventually began reflecting on what she had said. Somewhere deep inside of me, I realized that her comment could only take power if I created a story that would let it take power. Instead, I asked the question, 'What can I really learn from this?'

It led me to start a conversation with myself and others – that helped me to progress. I learned that, from time to time, I was protective of my own reputation and sometimes fearful about revealing information that might have allowed others to help me. As a result, I portrayed a stance that may have come across as inconsistent. I learned more about my reactions to perceived 'authority figures'. I also learned that when people label, it's their issue; not mine. That's not to say they shouldn't be called out on it – because they should. When I believe it's truly their issue, a lot of emotion is taken out of it; I can be much more objective and call attention to the infringement in a more effective manner.

In summary, think about how you process valuable feedback others give you.

- Do you take conscious control?
- Do you prematurely dismiss it?
- Do you dig beneath the surface?
- Are you aware of the way you create the story? Or even aware of the fact that you create a story at all?
- Do you take the feedback to an identity story level inappropriately?
- Do you make the most of affirmational feedback others give you?

Receiving feedback is a creative skill – the art of making stories about yourself and the surrounding situation. In the penultimate chapter, we'll briefly look at the broader application of the Collaborative Feedback Model.

Recap

- Getting people to learn to process feedback more skilfully will avoid a lot of problems for your organization.
- It's important to be aware of how you process the feedback you're given.
- Be aware of the different types of internal stories you create – belief stories, identity stories and value stories. Be careful of how you create these.
- Decide to appreciate the feedback you are given. See it as a gift – always, even if it is poorly delivered. They're just not good at wrapping!
- Take control of the feedback you're given by getting to the intention and breaking down what is said to specifics.
- Take ownership for any feedback given using the Feedback Tool and dig for nuggets.

CHAPTER 9

MORE APPLICATIONS OF THE COLLABORATIVE FEEDBACK MODEL

In this chapter, we'll briefly look at some of the not-so-obvious applications of the principles that exist in the PRESENT Model of collaborative feedback. What do I mean by that? Well, we've been talking about feedback for the last eight chapters. Feedback mechanisms are everywhere. Lots of things that happen in organizations are dependent upon feedback mechanisms. The efficacy of communication is based on successful feedback. It, therefore, stands to reason that any processes that require feedback might benefit from the principles in the PRESENT Model. We'll explore this by applying the principles contained in the model along with an abbreviated version of the Preparation Tool and look at how it can help you in seven broader categories:

- Generating clarity
- Learning
- Selling or persuading
- Win-win negotiations
- Conflict resolution
- Challenging the status quo
- Self-development

You'll find that as we explore these, they are all linked.

Before we begin the exploration, you'll recall that the Collaborative Feedback Preparation Tool is comprised of five sentence starters. In this chapter, we'll focus on three of them (listed below). The first sentence starter – 'My outcome is...' – is, of course, crucial for determining the direction you want to take the conversation and the second – 'I'm currently feeling...' – is important for controlling your state but we'll take these as given, to focus on the other three. This will be the focus of our exploration. Let me remind you again of the last three sentence starters:

- I notice...
- And the meaning I make of that is...
- And that might mean...

A tool for generating clarity

So much of a successful business depends on its ability to produce clarity: on strategies, objectives, measurements, KPIs, standards, agreements, working relationships; the list goes on and on. Without clarity, you have misunderstandings, dashed expectations, stress and unnecessary problems. I can't tell you the number of times I've come out of meetings and got wildly differing versions (almost comical) of what was agreed. How do you then act on that? How do you then measure what was acted upon? Impossible. It just doesn't work.

Several years ago, I was conducting an exercise on objectives. In this organization, staff would define their own objectives for the year. Their managers would then input into the process, and they would together agree on the final set of objectives. Employees would then be measured against this on their annual appraisal, which then determined their bonus for the year. Probably not a surprise to you, as many organizations function this way. In this exercise, we got together separately with both the staff member and manager and got detailed about what these objectives meant and how they would be measured. The disparity in understanding was astonishing. How the staff member interpreted the objectives and how the manager interpreted was often significantly different. No wonder there were lots of difficult conversations during appraisal sessions - ending in the aftermath of resentment at the loss of bonuses.

Clarity is essential for the most basic things. Stuff gets done in an organization because somewhere, sometime, someone has a conversation with someone else. Without clarity, stuff gets done badly or not at all. But consider this, clarity itself is an iterative process of feedback. It goes something like this:

Information is given (feedback is presented) – information is processed – more information is gleaned – more information processed – until there is a shared understanding. It's a loop – a feedback loop.

I sit in lots of meetings where communication is predominantly one way, where feedback mechanisms don't kick in; people sit there and nod their heads or not, and the result is lack of clarity. In most cases, people just assume there is clarity and muddle their way through. In other cases, the lack of clarity results in extra meetings and work having to be redone.

Standards don't work without clarity; neither do agreements. So, it was no big surprise when I heard one of my program participants talk about a standard service agreement that wasn't working; they simply hadn't got enough clarity about what it meant or how it operated – or why it existed.

However, an abbreviated version of the Preparation Tool in Chapter 5 is excellent for driving clarity in a conversation. You can use its structure repeatedly to drive conversations to clarity. Also, remember what was covered in a previous chapter – sometimes people don't know what they mean until they say it.

Here's an example I picked up in a meeting recently. The senior management team had been deliberating over a decision that their managers had escalated to them. A couple of months later, there was still no resolution to the problem posed. I just happened to be facilitating the team meeting that day and played the abbreviated Collaborative Feedback Preparation Tool out in my mind.

I notice you said we needed to make this decision soon.

The meaning I make of that is that we are putting off the decision because we don't have a systematic way of making hard decisions or we're afraid of making it, in case it's the wrong decision

And that might mean you lose momentum and the faith of the staff as the problems continue.

It took a few seconds to run through the model and then I said, 'May I just bring up a point so that we get some clarity on what was discussed. I notice that no decision has yet been made – even though there has been lots of deliberation and we all agreed we need to make this decision soon. Is that because we don't know how to make the decision or that we are afraid of making the decision?'

I watched the response from the room and then added: 'I'm laying my thinking on the table – the reality may be different. Because if that's the case, I hear rumblings from the staff that the problems are worsening because of the lack of resolution. Am I missing anything?'

There followed a productive discussion on what 'soon' meant and why the decision was put off. We got more clarity regarding as to why the decision wasn't made. Shortly after, the decision was made.

Another example, which happened many moons ago, was a request from my former boss. At 4 p.m. on Friday afternoon, he called me into his office and asked for a report that would need to be handed in on Tuesday morning. Because I wanted to impress, I duly agreed. It wasn't until I got out of his office did my mental tirade begin. 'Idiot! (him not me) It's 4 p.m. on Friday afternoon. Why can't he do it himself? So disorganized! It's going to eat up most of my weekend. Why the hell did I agree to do it? Idiot! (Me, not him! – well – also him.) I wish I'd dared to say no. I'm so stupid. I need to find another job...' and so on and so on and so on.

I finally got around to doing the report, and after much sweat and tears and a weekend swallowed up, I handed in a beautifully typed up, complete with impressive graphics, 32-page report on Tuesday morning. As I handed it to him, inwardly expecting a 'Thank you so much for your commitment and effort' he said, 'Oh, I was expecting a one-pager. Do you think you can shorten it?'

'DOH! Idiot, idiot, idiot!'

If only I'd applied the Collaborative Feedback Model in my mind at that time to generate more clarity on what was expected.

I notice you say 'report'.

The meaning I'm making of this is that you are looking for a 32-page report that is well presented.

And that might mean it takes up all my weekend to do it.

I then might have said something like, 'Can I just check for clarity? You're looking for a detailed report, roughly about 30 pages that is well presented?'

To which he would have replied, 'Oh God no. One page will be fine.'

It would have saved me so much suffering, but it was a lesson well learned. Imagine if we were to have these conversations with our clients and colleagues at work, how much more clarity would be generated, leading to more efficient, more pleasant working.

Use the Collaborative Feedback Preparation Tool to generate clarity. When you run it mentally, it will increase the chances of you uncovering assumptions you are making regarding the situation. When you test and retest the assumptions in conversation, you get closer to clarity. Additionally, get into the habit of trying to visualize what they are saying.

When you encounter language that you can't see or hear internally, question it to get further clarification.

A tool for learning

In our work, we are continually learning. We are learning new processes, new software, new ways of thinking, new tools, working with different types of individuals, new innovations, new relationships. We're learning whether we know it or not. It's just that some people learn quicker and better than others. And we haven't even started on the stuff outside of work. Those that learn quicker, somehow make the connections that matter, faster and adapt quicker. It makes sense that anything we can do to help us learn better is of deep importance because it will affect our lives in so many ways.

I'm aware that we learn in all kinds of ways and with different styles – consciously and subconsciously. However, most work learning involves making meaning of the information that we are presented with, applying it and reapplying with adjustments. Learning itself is an iterative process. Any iterative process suggests feedback and guess what? That's where the abbreviated Collaborative Feedback Preparation Tool comes in useful.

Now, I've taken up a couple of hobbies which I want to get better at – snooker and tennis. Both skills are highly technical and require intensive practice by trial and error if I am to reach the levels to which I aspire (which incidentally is not very high). I've had the fortune of finding two fabulous mentors in both these fields. Paul Bishop is an ex-professional on the ATP Tennis Tour and a highly gifted coach and entrepreneur. James is a young 21-year-old snooker player, who's been playing since the age of 10 and regularly scores breaks of 100-plus.

Both have taken the time to give me instruction on what it takes to improve, which I am deeply grateful for. What's interesting is underneath any instruction or hint there is a plethora of deeper information that allows the skill to develop and flourish. What's even more interesting is they don't even know it's there until it's somehow tapped into. Any complex skill comprises of deep layers of other stuff (beliefs, values, physical adjustments, knowledge) that enables it to live at its current level. Unfortunately, these layers are buried below consciousness in most cases. The more talented teachers, coaches, mentors know how to tap into these, but unfortunately, these few are not always available.

Think of the most skilful of salespeople or negotiators or coders or engineers or any operator for that matter. They will tell you that what they do is simple to them, but when you try and emulate what they do, you'll discover that what they do is multi-layered in so many ways. It's simple to them because they've practised these layers until each one has merged into simple strands. They then tell you what they do is 'simple', because it feels simple to them. If you could get between those layers, you would learn so much faster and more completely. Think of it like mining for gold in the gold rush days. You must keep digging with the shovel. And if your shovel isn't fit for purpose, you'll have a hard time uncovering the gold. Is there a tool that is akin to a shovel for learning? You bet. The Collaborative Feedback Preparation Tool.

I'll give you an example from both snooker and tennis to illustrate how these have helped me personally.

Tennis example

> TENNIS COACH: You've got to keep hitting the ball much higher over the net, and the ball will get deeper and deeper, and your opponent will get pushed back more and more. Then you'll begin to feel it.

At this point, I ran the preparation tool inside my mind.
I noticed he used the word 'feel' and he seemed to emphasize it with his tone.
The meaning I make of that is there's much more to the word 'feel', and I don't really get what he's talking about.
And that might mean I'm missing something important that might level up my game.
So, I continued the conversation:

> CHRIS: I just want to get a bit more clarity on what you

said. When you said 'feel' I get a sense that it's essential – is that right?

TENNIS COACH: Oh, yes, that's key to everything. Tennis is all about the feel. You're continually looking for the feel.

CHRIS: What do you mean by that?

And we had the most wonderful conversation about 'feel' where I was able to pick his brain based on 20 years of hard drilled practice. It helped me to know where to put my attention and focus as I practised.

<u>Snooker example</u>

SNOOKER MENTOR: Make sure you time the ball right. It will help you strike the ball more cleanly.

Once again, I ran the preparation tool inside my head.
I noticed he used the word 'time' and 'cleanly' and I cannot picture what that looks like.
The meaning I make of that is that it's vitally important, but there's a big gap in my knowledge because I can't break down what he's saying.
And that might mean I will never strike the ball cleanly.
So, I asked.

CHRIS: I hear you saying the word timing and hitting the ball cleanly. In my mind, that's a big blank. Do you mean I've got to be more deliberate in the way I hit it?

SNOOKER MENTOR: Partly, but it's more than that. It's about pausing at the backswing, hitting it deliberately but in a way that the arm is relaxed. You'll know you've timed it well because of the sound of the balls connecting.

That led to me enquiring what a good sound sounded like versus a bad sound, and now I have a feedback mechanism for whether I'm timing the ball well or not. It's helped my game enormously.

You'll probably have noticed in my examples; I keep repetitiously using the Preparation Tool. And some of you may be asking, 'But can't you just ask questions on words that you don't understand? That's what you're doing anyway. Why bother with the model? Isn't it overkill?' I'm glad you asked.

Yes, you're absolutely right. That's what will eventually happen anyway. But for those who aren't yet adept at this stuff, we're trying to build a scaffold that will continually reinforce the concept that there is a story and it's just your story. My goal is that by the end of the book, you'll have run the model lots of times, enough to have learned it and be able to run it without relooking. I promise it will help you.

Innovation and learning in the workplace

So how does this apply in the workplace?

In today's business climate, we must continuously innovate, which requires us to learn and improve so many skills in so many areas. The Preparation Tool can help speed up learning in any of these areas. It will help you to glean more from trainers, mentors, and skilful practitioners alike.

All training is incomplete because the model of how to do something well is usually much more complex than what is presented. Likewise, the knowledge imparted from your mentors is also incomplete because, as I mentioned, their knowledge is built up of layers and layers of experience, which they have long since forgotten. They only remember pieces of a bigger essential jigsaw puzzle. You need to get these little bits of information – distinctions if you like, that will help you have a better model of how the skill is done. The same is true for organizational best practice.

Here's an example in the workplace that happened between a close colleague, Iyare, and me. Iyare is a highly skilful facilitator and can capture the attention of a large room very quickly. And nearly every group engages with him – immediately and with lots of laughter and fun. It's quite something to see him in action! That's gold to any facilitator and to any leader. He has their attention and engagement, and they love him! I had to find out how he did it. I observed him. I also asked him how he did it. This was part of the conversation:

CHRIS: How do you get the room energized so quickly and people laughing, having fun and completely engaged.

IYARE: It's about your tone and pace. When you focus on your voice and how you can vary your tone and pace, the rest follows.

CHRIS: Yes, I've noticed that. You slow it right down, and then you speed it up. However, I also notice that you engage in conversation with one individual and then engage again with the larger group and then zoom into another individual. I'm guessing that's an important part of the engagement piece. Is that right?

IYARE: Oh, yes. Very important. You have to be present for people.

CHRIS: I also notice that you make things more personal by using lots of metaphors.

IYARE: Yes, personify and exaggerate. That's everything. That's partly how you get them to play.

> CHRIS: So, to get people into a place where they begin to play, you take examples and language and personify concepts and exaggerate as you go along.
>
> IYARE: Partly. First, you must believe that they will play with you. When I engage with them, I don't have any doubt that they will play.

And the more I used the Preparation Tool to break down what I noticed and fed it back to Iyare, the more knowledge came out. Iyare's skill is complex, but he thinks it's simple. However, when you break it down, you realize there are layers. If you want to emulate his results, you have to get the bits out that makes the difference. I began to practice what I was learning from my highly skilled colleague and was overjoyed when I was able to replicate some of his results with a large group a month later.

Later Iyare admitted that he had no idea of how he did what he did and that he found it immensely useful that I had fed back my observations. It also gave him vital information that allowed him to improve his skills even further.

I know you might be asking, 'But why not just ask the trainer or mentor or skilful practitioner questions? Why do you have to go through the rigmarole of the Preparation Tool?'

And it's a good question and here's where the value lies. I've spent nearly two decades training various management skills. From a trainer's point of view, when I train, it doesn't matter how much information I present, either in an interactive form or any other format, I have very little idea of how you are processing the information. Maybe you're getting what I'm saying exactly; maybe you're not. I have no idea what goes in and what doesn't. If I knew where the gaps were, I could really help. If I don't know, I guess.

Also, sequencing is important. If the sequence in your mind of what must be done to learn the skill is suboptimal, the results might also be suboptimal. However, to communicate this information to me, you must be able to have a clear idea of the meaning-making process in your mind. This is where the Preparation Tool comes in. Your use of the tool gives me a story on which to build upon or challenge to help you get to the right place. If you were simply to ask the question, I still wouldn't have any idea what story is forming in your mind and could be focusing my answers in the wrong place.

As a learner, you'll also probably sometimes assume we share a common understanding, when in fact we don't. But if you lay your thinking on the table, I can see where your gaps are. That's why teaching back a topic is great for learning. You are essentially laying your thinking on the table.

When we truly collaborate as the giver of knowledge and experience and learner of knowledge and experience, we get the transfer so much quicker.

Sometimes I use the Preparation Tool as a learning tool explicitly – I run through the model before we begin the training and ask the group to use the tool to feedback what they are learning as they are learning it. It gives great insight into how knowledge is being assimilated, leading to better results.

Armed with the knowledge of these principles, you can mine for any knowledge or skills that will help you take things to the next level. Take responsibility and ownership for your learning. Don't let your learning be dependent on the skill of the teacher, mentor, trainer, coach! You uncover the layers by using the Preparation Tool.

A tool for selling and persuasion

To be good at selling, we must be good at feedback. We all sell every day. Everyone is a type of salesperson – it's just that some aren't very good at it. You want your ideas to be taken on board, don't you? That's selling. You want a promotion or a better job? That involves selling yourself. You want your kids to eat vegetables? That involves sales. Any decent selling process is filled with small feedback processes. Various parts of the selling cycle – finding out needs or problems, handling objections, even closing – all involve finding out more information and expanding it to find solutions. That's where the Feedback Tool comes in handy. Usually, to make a sale with no buyer remorse, your customer or client has to feel like you fully understand their problem or desire and have a solution that fits within the parameters of their mind. To get there, you must tease the information out.

Here's why the Collaborative Feedback Preparation Tool is handy for selling. Because it's great for expanding the needs and problems your product or service could potentially solve – you then get a fuller picture of the types of issues facing the customer and what they want. And because you are laying your thinking on the table for your customer to see, it enables them to fill in the missing gaps. It also builds trust – and without trust, it's hard to close any sale. Just a few days ago, I used the tool during a sales conversation with a client regarding some consultancy. We were at the closing stage.

CHRIS: So, we've discussed it at length. Are we good to go?

CLIENT: Yes... I think so.

At this point, I sensed something, and the Feedback Tool kicked in
I noticed her tone was different.
The meaning I make of that is that there was hesitancy.
And that might mean she's worried about the risk and the political ramifications if she hasn't got it quite right. In her culture, making mistakes could have big consequences.
So, I continued the conversation:

> CHRIS: Did I detect a slight hesitancy in your tone? Can I take a stab and you can put me right? I'm sure I won't get it all correct, but you can set me straight. [Building safety.] I'll just put my thinking down for us to explore. [Communicating it's just my story.] I'm thinking that perhaps it might feel a bit risky to go for this type of approach without checking with the people who sit in this department. Does that resonate? And perhaps there needs to be another step before we fully sign off?
>
> CLIENT: Yes, I think you are right. We have to be really careful here.

And the client went on to explain some of the political nuances in the organization. We were then able to create an extra step which involved more senior characters, which eventually resulted in an increase in sales above the original proposal.

Some of you seasoned professionals may be asking, 'But why not just ask the client, instead of guessing – by laying your thinking on the table?' The reason is, sometimes people don't necessarily know the answers because there's too much happening at the subconscious level. But when you present your thinking to them, with the caveat you know you may be making assumptions, it gives them data in which to start processing their own thinking. They know what they like or what they don't like, what is accurate and what is inaccurate and soon insights come to their minds. And don't underestimate the power that the building of trust plays when they see your thinking is transparent.

Much of sales is about unearthing and creating stories. The Feedback Tool can help you to find the stories that genuinely help your customers. (Although, I say all this with the caveat that your products or services must be able to genuinely help your customers or clients in the first place.)

As a salesperson, you collaborate with your customer or client to co-create value and the Collaborative Feedback Preparation Tool helps you to do it.

A tool for a win-win negotiation

There are roughly two types of negotiation philosophies that I see used in business; positional negotiation and collaborative negotiation. (Don't quote me on this. For the purists among you, I'm sure that you can find ways to further categorize.) Often a blend of the two is used.

Positional negotiation is based upon parties taking positions and gradually coming to a compromise. When you think of hardball negotiating, this is the type of negotiation it's based upon. The simple form of this is haggling. I remember negotiating the price tag of my first car as a youngster:

CHRIS: I like it. How much do you want for the car?

CAR SELLER: £2,500.

CHRIS: I can give you £1,500.

CAR SELLER: What?! Are you crazy? The car's in good condition, and that's way below what the price guide says.

CHRIS: That depends on what price guide you use. And it's dependent on whether you think it's in great or good condition. OK, how about £1,800?

CAR SELLER: £2,200.

CHRIS: Shall we split the difference – £2,000?

CAR SELLER: OK.

The proponents of positional negotiation often use tactics of hiding information, power bolstering, fronting, and the results often end as win-lose or lose-lose. Everyone compromises but no one gets what they really want.

I've seen a fair number of organizations employ primarily positional negotiation strategies with their service contractors who desperately want their business. And when they do this, a common pattern emerges. The contractors are driven low on price. They discover that the payoff for them against the work done isn't that great, and they aren't motivated to do their best. Quality of service falls, and often it's a lose-lose for everyone.

Hard positional negotiation can be advantageous if it's a one-off transaction, but if you want to have a long-term relationship with the other party, think carefully about how hard you drive it. Collaborative negotiation is based upon parties not negotiating on positions but on interests. You get past the positions that parties take, lay your interests on the table and try and create a variety of different solutions that end up benefitting everyone. It's going for a win-win. It's also co-creation.

In *Getting to Yes: Negotiating an agreement without*

Giving In (a fabulous book for this type of negotiation) Fisher, Ury and Patton argue that it can still be tough, but it leads to sustainable results for everyone. They talk about avoiding the 'zero-sum game 'by not bargaining over positions, separating people from the problems, inventing options for mutual gain and insisting on using objective criteria in the event of a deadlock. To do this, you have to have the courage to be much more transparent in your thinking. But it's not only being transparent, it's also how to do in such a way to not appear weak, inappropriate, irrelevant or in a way that doesn't increase unnecessary friction.

In today's business world, organizations realize that collaborative negotiation should play a much bigger role. This is because there is so much more at stake, given the shrinking landscape due to globalization and technological advances. The internet has enabled knowledge to spread much wider and faster. Secrets are much harder to keep, and businesses are finding it harder to keep their competitive advantage. Hard positional negotiation can end up making you seem outdated, incompetent and untrustworthy. We are so much more interconnected.

But there's a problem when you want to use collaborative negotiation, and that's the reason why *Getting to Yes* devotes two whole chapters to the topic. Others who aren't familiar or who don't buy into collaborative negotiation won't necessarily play the collaborative negotiation game. You, as the practitioner, must convert the game from a positional negotiation to a collaborative negotiation. And you have to find practical ways of doing this – use language that does this and often under potentially stressful situations. You want to get behind the position, but you don't want to unnecessarily offend the other party in doing so.

And this is where the Preparation Tool in conjunction with the PRESENT Model comes in: it gives you a systematic way of laying down a story for people to examine, in a non-combative way, even if the situation is potentially conflict-filled.

An example comes to mind from a few years back. I was talking with a client regarding a piece of work – training leadership skills. We had gotten to the fun part – talking money and budgets. I thought I had painstakingly laid out the value proposition – the benefits against the costs – and thought I had done a good job. But then the client took a position on the cost.

> CLIENT: It sounds really good and just what we're looking for. However, I can't go any higher than £40,000 – our budget doesn't allow it. If you take it, then it's yours. If you don't, then we can't do it.

At this point, I felt a bit dazed. I felt really tempted to accept the offer, yet that was quite a bit below my initial offer. Then the principles of Collaborative Feedback kicked into play.

I notice he gave me an 'either or offer' with a particular tone.

The meaning I make of that is it puts a pressure on me to take it. Otherwise, we get into conflict, and he's playing a kind of positional negotiating game based upon his perception of the situation.

And that means it's a loser for me and possibly a longer-term 'lose' for both of us and that we are not exploring other options.

Articulating the story inside my head gave me a way to express myself in a favourable way going forward. I continued...

> CHRIS: I notice we are focusing on price and I'm thinking

we are getting ourselves into an either/or situation. That means we're unable to explore other possibilities, which might give us both a much better deal and I'd really like to do that. Does that seem a fair summation?

CLIENT: What do you mean – other possibilities?

And we continued to talk. As it turned out, the client also needed other urgent management development, and as the leadership modules were half-a-day, I could spend the other half-day working with the team to put that into place. I was there anyway, and it enabled both our interests to be met. He needed other management development, and I needed cash flow without expending extra days. Win-win!

The real power of using the principles is it enables you to articulate the story, lay your thinking on the table and expose the games that are being played, in a non-confrontational manner. Why is it non-confrontational? Because it's just your story and you've communicated it as such.

A tool for conflict resolution

At the heart of the Collaborative Feedback Model is laying your stories on the table for others to examine. This lends itself well to conflict resolution. Conflict occurs because people are locked into stories. The real skill of conflict resolution is taking everyone's stories and expanding the context. As they see the much bigger picture, parties realize other things are important, that are temporarily unsighted.

A classic example is gang wars. Killing leads to hurt, and the need for revenge, which only propagates the cycle and the conflict escalates. Until the gang members see and feel the bigger picture, they don't realize everyone loses – big time! The problem is because there is conflict, tension is at a high and conversations can explode into an impasse. The Collaborative Feedback Model has safety and honesty built into its DNA. By laying your story out and exploring others' stories, it paves the way for context to expand and conflict to dissipate.

A tool for challenging the status quo

From time to time, it's necessary to challenge the status quo. We live in a fast-moving world and, unless we innovate, we'll soon be left behind. You can't innovate unless you question the status quo. Processes could be more efficient or effective; relationships could be improved; established ways of working could be challenged. However, challenging the status quo is often tricky. Those who set up the current system can take the challenge personally. Those who don't like change can provide resistance. You have to lay the challenge down skilfully to get useful discussions that lead to innovation and change.

As a professional facilitator, part of my job is to challenge the status quo. Can we get better? Can we be even more efficient? Is he or she in the way? Are meetings being run efficiently? Is the decision-making process working the way we want it to?

A participant on my program shared an example he had come across – and it was something I had also witnessed on many occasions in the boardroom. He was a board member and noticed in meetings, someone would table a decision. The chairman would then offer an opinion, and because he was a powerful personality, everyone else just agreed. The participant then used the Feedback Tool to bring notice to this by saying, 'I'm just noticing we are in the habit of tabling a decision and, more often than not, our illustrious chairman offers an opinion that everyone else follows – or at least that's how it seems to me – I might be wrong. I then have conversations outside of the meeting, which hint that others are not entirely fully on board with the decisions we've reached. As a result, things get done half-heartedly. Surely that means we're not using our diversity to make even more robust decisions.'

The chairman agreed, and things changed. (Nice bit of irony)

A tool for personal development

We'll finish this chapter by looking at how the Collaborative Feedback Model can be immensely helpful for your personal development. We've already explored it in the context of learning, and personal development is, of course, a type of learning. But it is especially helpful because the model gives you a way to consciously break down your own stories. As we explored in Chapter 8, our stories can limit what's possible for us and what's not. We already looked at how belief stories and value stories drive our own thinking and behaviour. And we've also explored how beliefs and values are woven into the fabric of our identity stories. And it's when things begin to shift and change at these levels, that we experience growth leaps and wild new possibilities.

The principles in the PRESENT Model and the Preparation Tool enables you to systematically bring your belief stories into consciousness and provides a way for you to break down and reconstruct them. It's a powerful self-awareness tool. Here's an example of how it helped me.

In my work with leadership teams, part of my role is to take them to their own limitations and then go beyond them; to explore what's possible. Something that really helps this type of work is taking them into a playful space where banter, humour and enjoyment enable them to laugh at themselves and thus explore more unreservedly. I know what helps create this space is the way I role model as the facilitator of that experience. There are times when I could say and do things that take them there, but I am hesitant and decide to be more cautious in the name of appropriateness. As a result, I feel led when I should be leading. This frustrates me but also gives me an insight into my own stories as to where I believe can go and where I can't. I encounter my own limitations. I used the Preparation Tool to bring the story into awareness so that I could examine it, explore it and find ways to test and push those boundaries.

Here's how I used the tool:

I notice that when the group is not smiling, or quieter than usual, I hold back by lowering my tones and using more logical language rather than playful language.

The meaning I make of that is that it's inappropriate to be playful when others are serious or quiet. I, therefore, don't have the right. If I am playful in this environment, they will think I am unprofessional, and I will feel foolish.

And that means there are certain things I cannot do in our time together, and we can't have some types of experiences that will make a deeper impact.

As I held my statements to the 'light of truth', I realized the story I had created and was continuing to create. Why can't I be playful when others 'seem' serious – and for a lot of leadership teams, seriousness is their default state of being. Does that mean I need to be the same? The very reason I am invited to work with these teams is to help them develop different ways of being. What would it be like to be out there on my own being playful? What does it say about how I should be in the presence of others? In the presence of powerful people?

This helped me then create a different story and thus, a different reality. It's OK to be the only one being playful for a while. It's my role to take them to a playful place and not to just conform to the group. It's an expectation from them and from me. They are waiting for me to take them there.

Now, will this immediately change the belief? After all, I might feel the same the next time it happens? And it's our feelings that indicate the true beliefs that we hold. Well no, it might not change it immediately, but it gives us options to explore and try different things.

As a result of this newfound awareness, I was able to have a conversation with a close friend and colleague who also works in leadership development. He has a belief when working with a large group that goes something like this: 'We will have a fabulous time together laughing, joking and playing together. You will love me, and I will love you.'

What a belief to hold every time he delivers a leadership workshop! As a result, he goes into work full of confidence, fully resourceful and looking forward to the day. And guess what? People love him and the work he does. And this led me to the insight of, 'Why don't I try and hold that belief as I am about to deliver?'

So, the next few sessions, I consciously ran that story in my mind, just before we were about to start. Did it make a difference? Sometimes. Sometimes not, but I can already feel a difference in how I was before. And I truly believe it's only a matter of time before that belief settles comfortably into the core of my being.

The principles held in the PRESENT Model of collaborative feedback and its Preparation Tool allows you to begin to process your belief and value stories in a systematic, conscious way – which can then lead toward different possibilities in life.

I hope you've seen from this chapter, the many different uses of the Collaborative Feedback Preparation Tool. I hope I've demonstrated how useful these principles are – in lots of different business contexts. My program participants often comment they naturally use them anyway but in an unconscious manner. By bringing it into your consciousness and by practice and refinement, it can help in so many situations. My hope is you will begin to experiment with them in new and different ways.

Recap

- The PRESENT Model of Collaborative Feedback and its Preparation Tool can be applied in many business contexts.
- Use them to generate clarity in all types of conversations.
- The model can be applied to enhance learning.
- They're useful in selling and situations where you want to influence.
- They're helpful in negotiation situations.
- They're helpful for conflict resolution.
- The principles are helpful for personal development.

CONCLUSION

DEVELOPING A CULTURE OF COLLABORATIVE FEEDBACK

In the previous chapters, we've explored how giving more feedback (both adjustment and affirmational), in a manner more likely to end in collaboration, is essential in creating successful relationships throughout your home and work life. Finally, I'd like to spend a short time exploring what it takes to develop a culture of Collaborative Feedback in our organizations.

First, we need to understand that embracing the benefits of Collaborative Feedback – both adjustment and affirmational – can only be positive because we are undoubtedly better together. In particular, organizations must be 'together' and aligned to deliver their value propositions effectively and efficiently. One-way communication simply won't cut it. If you're in a leadership position, you'll understand that one-way communication leads to disengagement, misunderstanding and confusion.

With great regularity someone, somewhere in an organization, will look at me and make a comment, 'We're not very good at communication are we?' The question suggests the problem is easy to solve, and they have somehow failed.

To which I always reply, 'In every organization I work with – and I mean every – a version of this problem exists. Every organization struggles with communication.'

Communication is complex, even between individuals, and when you multiply that by X, you have issues. Collaborative Feedback is a way of getting clarity out of that complexity.

Also, if we lack confidence in giving tricky feedback, we will always have gaps in our processes and have problems delivering strategy. This will result in increased work you generate for yourself and others around you – further increasing costs and delivery of your propositions. And the list goes on. Collaborative adjustment feedback, if done well, gives people the confidence to challenge and co-create with their peers and those who report to them and to whom they report.

One vital piece of feedback, delivered at an apt moment, with skill, could change the destiny of an organization.

The value of Collaborative Feedback

A few years back, a former director of a large organization described how they'd had to radically downsize due to a wrong decision taken in a risky market. The decision was finely balanced and, ultimately, the say of the most powerful stakeholder, the CEO. Several of the other directors had reservations, but these were never fully explored because everyone felt too nervous about challenging power in the room.

Can you look into the future and begin to see that as employees lay out their thinking for their peers, leaders and others to see, in a respectful manner that offers up their own assumptions, how processes and relationships can improve? Trust is improved? Everyone is really heard? How valuable and empowering is that?

Imagine if employees at every level, engaged in collaborative affirmational feedback daily? How encouraging would it be to work in such an organization? How much more personal development would there be? Strengths recognized? Best practice regularly updated? Eyes lit up as the workforce felt genuinely appreciated? Fewer sick days? Reduced staff turnover? Less politicking? Leaders proud of their staff? Staff proud of their leaders. Employees wanting to go to work, knowing they will be recognized for all their great strengths and efforts and truly appreciated. Can you see it? Can you feel it?

Gina was surprised that collaboration always trumped solo performance.

What will it take and what will happen?

One by one, every individual putting the principles into practice and becoming proficient at Collaborative Feedback. Being more and more aware of their own stories and others' stories and laying both out in plain sight. It's action that counts, not theory.

There's a fascinating and unsettling (for some) phenomenon that happens when someone gets good at Collaborative Feedback. They continue to lay out their own and others' behaviours for all to see in a deeply respectful way. Political games are much harder to play: there's no getting away with muddy thinking. And it's hard to resist when someone lays their thinking on the table – because there's no resistance coming back. Why? Because they're too bothered about going back and re-laying safety. How can you have a one-way fight? Behaviours get exposed. Thinking gets exposed. You get to see what's really happening much, much faster. It only takes someone with a wide network to have a special impact.

And if you're a leader, you have a special responsibility to model these behaviours. It's no use expecting others to be respectful and collaborative when you aren't displaying these same behaviours.

Leaders and managers (if such a distinction is real), start getting aware of your vocal tones and body language in communication and feedback situations and recognize the non-intentional 'power games' that are at play. Set extra safety and lay your own assumptions on the table for all to see. Give gifts all day long. Play Santa the whole year round. So long as it's genuine and specific, it will never get stale. Watch what happens as people grow and develop, and newer models of best practice in so many areas are made explicit.

Don't take my word for it. Experiment, practice, keep adjusting and watch what happens when you employ Collaborative Feedback in your interactions.

If you're a leader in the top team in your business, you know if you take it seriously and adopt a mindset of Collaborative Feedback, it will only be a matter of time before it trickles down. Because you're part of the top team, there's implicit accountability. As you start to give feedback about the way feedback is given and received, it will begin to change. And because you're inviting others into a two-way conversation about it, it will begin to change even more.

Make Collaborative Feedback part of your recruitment process, part of your induction expectations and part of your appraisal process.

If you're a manager, have regular conversations with your direct reports about how feedback should be given and received in the work environment. And if you're managed by someone and they don't bring it up, make sure you do. It's very powerful when managers and reports have an explicit and shared understanding of how they conduct their relationships. You know for a fact that you're going to annoy one another from time to time. Agree on what happens when you are annoyed and how this is resolved between you – before it happens.

All these things work towards instilling a culture of Collaborative Feedback. Good luck with your journey to a more effective, efficient and pleasant work culture.

Final thoughts

Thank you so much for taking the time out to read this book; it's an honour that you have chosen to do so. Together we've explored the concept of Collaborative Feedback, the PRESENT Model and its associated Collaborative Feedback Preparation Tool and its many applications. In some ways, what we've been talking about is, at its heart, very simple:

- Be aware of your own stories.
- Lay your thinking for all to see.
- Give feedback that compellingly invites others to engage.

I hope you find the PRESENT Model and its associated Preparation Tool simple and easy to use. You'll find that you won't always remember to utilize the principles – this is the case even with me and my program participants, but when you do, you'll find that it will add quality to your feedback and make a difference to your life.

Play around with the PRESENT Model and feel free to experiment with it. Remember the Preparation Tool is a mental tool and not for verbal regurgitation. Once you've processed the situation via the tool, change your language to get the results you are looking for (see also the Appendix for more help to do this).

Finally, I believe that delivering feedback collaboratively has the power to transform lives, families, work cultures and communities. It is, in a sense, a plea to humanity to deeply respect one another and learn about the huge diversity that makes us human beings. If our work environments reflected this, it would enable the creation of so much more value, goodwill and happy living.

I hope you've enjoyed the book and found it useful. Good luck with your feedback journeys.

APPENDIX I

Below are some alternative phrases to express your feedback after you've processed it:

My outcome is...

- I just wanted to... (clarify the situation, get on the same page, clear expectations going forward, agree on some standards)
- I'm trying to...
- For the purpose of...

I notice...

- I see.../I saw...
- I heard you say...
- I observed...
- When you said...
- When you... [state the specific observation]

The meaning I make of that is...

- The way I'm processing that is...
- That makes me think...
- So, I'm guessing...
- So, as a result of that, I'm thinking...
- So, the story I'm creating in my mind is...

And that might mean...

- And the consequence, if that's true, is...
- And, as a result...
- And that might cause...

Alternative phrases to build safety and communicate it's only your story

- I might be wrong...
- I'm probably assuming some things...
- Let me lay my thinking on the floor/table for you to examine...
- This is just my perspective...
- This is just a perspective among others...
- I'm just having a stab at this...

REFERENCES

1. Prospect Theory: An analysis of Decision under Risk - Amos Tversky and Daniel Kahneman Econometrica Vol 47, No.2 (March 1979)
2. Study initially conducted by Pavlov Pavlov, I.P. [1955] Selected works
3. *Scientific American*, May 1957

ACKNOWLEDGEMENTS

I want to thank a few people who have been instrumental in the writing of this book.

Lin Manuel Miranda, the creator of Hamilton – which was played hundreds of times on loop as this book was created and edited.

To David Lewis for his brilliant Illustrations – his talent and speed of work is so amazing.

My friend, Matthew Taylor, who has given me valuable feedback and insight regarding the structure of the book.

Also, Iyare Umweni, an incredibly skilled and inspirational colleague; without our countless hours of conversations, insights, testing and retesting, this book wouldn't have been possible.

To Obi Abuchi and Mike Desouza, who helped massively in shaping my thinking regarding the model and especially Mike who took great pains to go through the drafts meticulously.

To Susannah (my wife's amazing friend), Magdalen (my sister), Georgia and Sarah who gave invaluable insight to make the book more appealing to a wider audience.

To the many, many participants on my feedback programs who have provided countless examples of field testing – for their honesty and for their courage in trying different things.

To my brilliant editor, Sandy, without her help, this book wouldn't have been possible. To my fabulous cover and interior designer, Charlotte for making the book look good.

To my children, Michael and Nyah, who have shown me with brutal honesty when it works and when it doesn't.

And finally, to my wonderful wife of many years, Karen, for her eternal support, her natural insights, her wit in challenging me when I violate my own feedback principles and her wisdom and deeply listening ear.

Made in the USA
Middletown, DE
11 August 2021